W9-AUA-884

BOSTON Herald

NEW ENGLAND
PATRIOTS
2004 SUPER BOWL
CHAMPIONS

SP
SPORTS
PUBLISHING
L.L.C.

www.SportsPublishingllc.com

PUBLISHER
Peter L. Bannon

SENIOR MANAGING EDITORS
Susan M. Moyer
Joseph J. Bannon Jr.

DEVELOPMENTAL EDITORS
Erin Linden-Levy
Elisa Bock Laird

ART DIRECTOR
K. Jeffrey Higgerson

IMAGING
Christine Mohrbacher and
Kenneth J. O'Brien

BOOK DESIGN, LAYOUT
Jennifer L. Polson

COVER DESIGN
Joseph Brumleve

COPY EDITOR
Cynthia L. McNew

PHOTO EDITOR
Erin Linden-Levy

PRESIDENT AND PUBLISHER
Patrick J. Purcell

EDITOR
Andrew F. Costello

SPORTS EDITOR
Rusty Hampton

EXECUTIVE SPORTS EDITOR
Mark Torpey

DIRECTOR OF PHOTOGRAPHY
Jim Mahoney

VICE PRESIDENT/PROMOTION
Gwen Gage

CHIEF LIBRARIAN
John Cronin

© 2004 *Boston Herald*
All Rights Reserved.

No part of this book may be reproduced in any form or by any electronic or
mechanical means including information storage and retrieval systems —
except in the case of brief quotations embodied in critical articles or reviews —
without permission in writing from its publisher, Sports Publishing L.L.C.
Except where otherwise noted, all stories and photographs are from the files of the *Boston Herald*.

Front cover photo: Michael Seamans/Boston Herald
Back cover photo: Kuni Takahashi/Boston Herald

Printed in the United States.

ISBN: 1-58261-790-2

www.SportsPublishingllc.com

Mi ha l! ama slE osto H ralc

Matthew We tlE t n He alc

PUBLISHER'S NOTE

Dear Friends,

It was only two seasons ago that a plucky group of overachievers won a wild card berth in the NFL playoffs and made an improbable march into the history books. Led by a baby-faced quarterback named Tom Brady, coach Bill Belichick & Co. shocked the world when they defeated the heavily favored St. Louis Rams in Super Bowl XXXVI in New Orleans.

In the 2003-2004 season, it was the same cast with a different script—the overachievers became overpowering.

Belichick, Brady and the Patriots were again on center stage, but much had changed in two years. The Cinderella kids had been transformed. No longer wide-eyed and star-struck, the 2003-2004 Patriots played with the intensity and fury of grizzled NFL veterans.

Once again led by Brady and a swarming defense, the Pats reeled off 15 consecutive victories and defeated the Carolina Panthers in Super Bowl XXXVIII in Houston. When the smoke cleared, all the experts agreed: The New England Patriots are the new dynasty on the American sports scene.

As was the case in 2002, the *Boston Herald*'s award-winning team of reporters and photographers was on hand to supply our readers with the most incisive, eye-catching coverage of the march to Houston and the ensuing Super Bowl triumph.

We hope you enjoy this commemorative collection, which celebrates the achievements of New England's top two teams—the Patriots and the *Boston Herald* staff.

Purcell

Patrick J. Purcell
President and Publisher
Boston Herald

Panel 1 (top-left)

Sports

Sox' bubble bursts in NY
Still 2½ back after loss to Yankees in series finale
Page 106

ALSO INSIDE
BRUINS OFFICIALLY OPEN
Page 88
Boston Uncommon ... 90
Revolution 94
Schools 75, 74

Paying the Bills

Belichick's move backfires as Patriots fall flat in opener
Story, Page 124

TABLES TURN: Bills safety Lawyer Milloy whoops it up after Buffalo's 31-0 victory over the Patriots left coach Bill Belichick and quarterback Tom Brady searching for answers.

SBLI No Nonsense Life Insurance
Now you need it more than ever — kind of like sleep
Lucky for you, it's easier to get!
$200,000 COVERAGE $10.09 month
1-888-GET-SBLI SBLI

WELCOME BACK STUDENTS
$0 TO JOIN

Panel 2 (top-center)

Sports

No easy ride for Red Sox
Wild card leaders wary after 7-2 loss to Chicago
Page 100

ALSO INSIDE
JIMMIE JOHNSON MAKES
Page 86
RON BURTON, the Patriots
Page 102

Kids are all right

Patriots come together for blowout victory over Eagles

NFL Week 2 SCOREBOARD

LOVE IN THE AIR: Patriots coach Bill Belichick rushes to greet defensive backs Asante Samuel (center) and Eugene Wilson after a big play during yesterday's 31-10 victory over the Eagles at Lincoln Financial Field in Philadelphia.

WELCOME BACK STUDENTS
$0 TO JOIN
SAVE $149

Panel 3 (top-right)

Sports

Pedro rights Red Sox' ship
Martinez erases memory of ugly loss
Page 98

U.S. women start strong
Hamm, Lilly star in Cup win over Sweden
Page 88

A bumpy flight

Patriots take off in win over Jets, but key players grounded   Story, Page 116

EVENTFUL JOURNEY: Patriots cornerback Asante Samuel catches his own deflection in front of coach Bill Belichick (top left) and then races 55 yards along the sideline before thrilling the Gillette Stadium crowd with what turned out to be the winning touchdown in yesterday's 23-16 victory over the New York Jets.

SBLI No Nonsense Life Insurance
Now you need it more than ever — kind of like sleep
Lucky for you, it's easier to get!
$200,000 COVERAGE $10.09 month
1-888-GET-SBLI SBLI

Panel 4 (middle-left)

Sports

Resiliency a Red Sox trait
Last at-bat loss to Tampa nothing new for this bunch
Page 102

ALSO INSIDE
BILL MUELLER BESTS
Manny Ramirez for the A.L. batting title.
Page 100

Capital offense

Patriots give away golden opportunity in loss to Washington   Story, Page 116

NFL Week 4 SCOREBOARD

JUST HANGING AROUND: Patriots quarterback Tom Brady tries to fend off Redskins defenders Jesse Armstead and Bruce Smith (right) as he looks for a receiver during yesterday's 20-17 loss to Washington in Landover, Md. Brady threw three interceptions in the game.

$1.00 TO JOIN!!!
Super Fitness

Panel 5 (middle-center)

GAME 5: THE TITANS

Pats get some attention

Grab key win vs. Titans before Sox-crazed crowd

By MICHAEL FELGER

RUBBING IT IN: Patriots defenders Matt Chatham, Jarvis Green and Tedy Bruschi celebrate a sack of Tennessee quarterback Steve McNair during yesterday's 38-30 win over the Titans at Gillette Stadium.

PILING ON: Patriots quarterback Tom Brady (top) joins the crowd celebrating Mike Cloud's third-quarter touchdown run yesterday at Gillette Stadium.

Panel 6 (middle-right)

GAME 6: THE GIANTS

Patriots, defense take

Beat New York, focus on Miami

By the numbers

FLYING HIGH: Pats defensive backs Asante Samuel (left) and Eugene Wilson celebrate after knocking down a pass during yesterday's 17-6 win over the New York Giants at Gillette Stadium.

Panel 7 (bottom-left)

Sports

Sox take look at Hoffman
Former shortstop first to get shot at manager job
Page 73

Candidates put to test
Interesting choice for skipper wannabes
Callahan, Page 62

Bronco busters

Brady, Pats overcome mistakes to pull out thrilling win   Story, Page 84

More Patriots

This setback really hurts
Pro Bowler Seymour at home with leg injury
Page 74

An outside perspective
Injured Johnson buoyed by newcomers' efforts
Mazur, Page 62

TARGET PRACTICE: Patriots quarterback Tom Brady prepares to let one fly during last night's 30-26 victory over the Denver Broncos. Brady, who threw for 350 yards, engineered a 58-yard scoring drive in the final minutes to secure the win.

ANC AMERICAN NUTRITION CENTER
718 Broadway, Everett, MA • 617-394-0678
anceverett.com
LOWEST PRICES ON THE WEB!!!
Free next day delivery*
Lose 10 lbs. for $29.95

Panel 8 (bottom-center)

Sports

Andover does swimmingly
Captures 5th straight title; soccer champs crowned
Pages 75-73

ALSO INSIDE
BRUINS KNOW FROM
experience that an early, successful start does not automatically mean much
Celtics 80-81
Colleges 84-76
Racing 62

Big 'D' for Pats

Belichick & Co. shut down Dallas, capture Bill Bowl   Story, Page 124

NFL Week 11 SCOREBOARD

GOOD STUFF: Patriots linebacker Tedy Bruschi (54) is corralled by teammates, including Richard Seymour (93) and Ty Law (right) after stopping Cowboys running back Troy Hambrick on a key fourth-down play in last night's 12-0 victory at Gillette Stadium.

Details, Pages 84-92, 68-69

SBLI No Nonsense Life Insurance
Now you need it more than ever — kind of like sleep
Lucky for you, it's easier to get!
$200,000 COVERAGE $10.09 month
1-888-GET-SBLI SBLI

Panel 9 (bottom-right)

Sports

Bumpy road for UMass
Minutemen in playoffs but Whipple rips process
Page 80

Earthquakes register win
San Jose beats Chicago to capture MLS Cup
Page 102

Escape artists

Patriots show their magic touch, rally for OT win over Texans
• Story, Page 124

1-2 PUNCH: Kicker Adam Vinatieri pumps his fist (above) as he watches the flight of his game-winning field goal in yesterday's 23-20 OT victory over the Texans — a win made possible by the play of Richard Seymour (93), Mike Vrabel and the defense (left).

T-Mobile 3-DAY WEEKEND
Unlimited calling on Friday, Saturday and Sunday
600 WHENEVER minutes
No long distance or roaming charges
$39.99 a month
Free Phone!!!

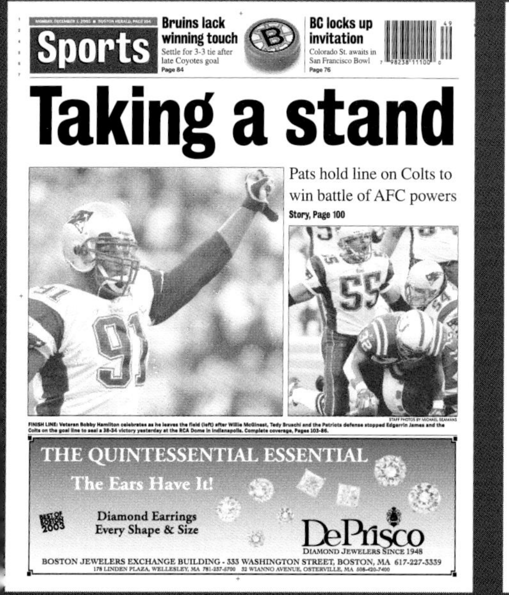
Sports

Bruins lack winning touch
Settle for 3-3 tie after late Coyotes goal
Page 84

BC locks up invitation
Colorado St. awaits in San Francisco Bowl
Page 76

Taking a stand

Pats hold line on Colts to win battle of AFC powers
Story, Page 100

STAFF PHOTOS BY MICHAEL SEAMANS

FINISH LINE: Veteran Bobby Hamilton celebrates as he leaves the field (left) after Willie McGinest, Tedy Bruschi and the Patriots defense stopped Edgerrin James and the Colts on the goal line to seal a 38-34 victory yesterday at the RCA Dome in Indianapolis. Complete coverage, Pages 103-86.

THE QUINTESSENTIAL ESSENTIAL
The Ears Have It!
BEST OF BOSTON 2003
Diamond Earrings
Every Shape & Size
DePrisco
DIAMOND JEWELERS SINCE 1948
BOSTON JEWELERS EXCHANGE BUILDING · 333 WASHINGTON STREET, BOSTON, MA 617-227-3339
178 LINDEN PLAZA, WELLESLEY, MA 781-237-2700 · 32 WIANNO AVENUE, OSTERVILLE, MA 508-420-7400

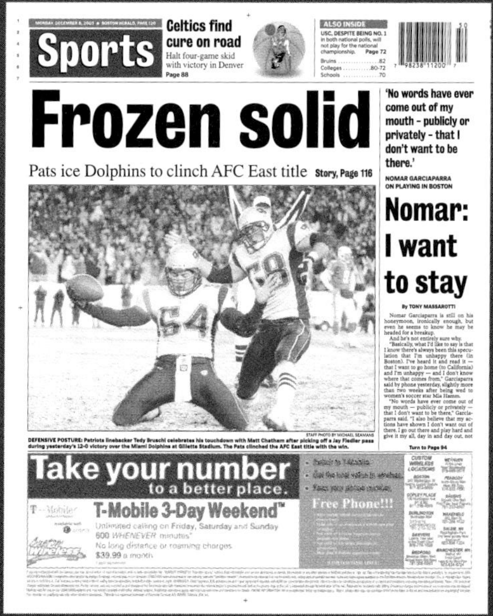
Sports

Celtics find cure on road
Halt four-game skid with victory in Denver
Page 88

ALSO INSIDE
USC, DESPITE BEING NO. 1 in both national polls, will not play for the national championship. Page 72
Bruins 82
Colleges 80-72
Schools 70

Frozen solid

Pats ice Dolphins to clinch AFC East title **Story, Page 116**

STAFF PHOTO BY MICHAEL SEAMANS

DEFENSIVE POSTURE: Patriots linebacker Tedy Bruschi celebrates his touchdown with Matt Chatham after picking off a Jay Fiedler pass during yesterday's 12-0 victory over the Miami Dolphins at Gillette Stadium. The Pats clinched the AFC East title with the win.

'No words have ever come out of my mouth - publicly or privately - that I don't want to be there.'
NOMAR GARCIAPARRA ON PLAYING IN BOSTON

Nomar: I want to stay

By TONY MASSAROTTI

Nomar Garciaparra is still on his honeymoon, ironically enough, but even he seems to know he may be headed for a breakup.

And he's not entirely sure why.

"Basically, what I'd like to say is that I know there's always been this speculation that I'm unhappy there (in Boston). I've heard it and read it — that I want to go home (to California) and I'm unhappy — and I don't know where that comes from," Garciaparra said by phone yesterday, slightly more than two weeks after being wed to women's soccer star Mia Hamm.

"No words have ever come out of my mouth — publicly or privately — that I don't want to be there," Garciaparra said. "I also believe that my actions have shown I don't want out of there. I go out there and play hard and give it my all, day in and day out, not

Turn to Page 94

Take your number to a better place.
T-Mobile 3-Day Weekend™
Unlimited calling on Friday, Saturday and Sunday
600 WHENEVER minutes
No long distance or roaming charges
$39.99 a month
Free Phone!!!

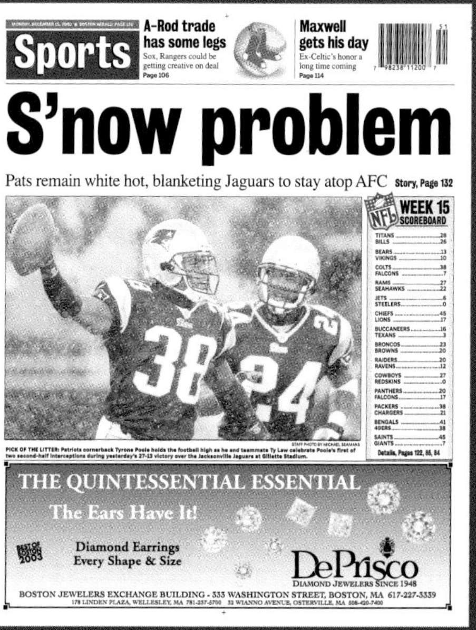
Sports

A-Rod trade has some legs
Sox, Rangers could be getting creative on deal
Page 106

Maxwell gets his day
Ex-Celtic's honor a long time coming
Page 114

S'now problem

Pats remain white hot, blanketing Jaguars to stay atop AFC **Story, Page 132**

NFL WEEK 15 SCOREBOARD

TITANS	28
BILLS	26
BEARS	13
VIKINGS	10
COLTS	38
FALCONS	7
RAMS	27
SEAHAWKS	22
JETS	6
STEELERS	0
CHIEFS	45
LIONS	17
BUCCANEERS	16
TEXANS	3
BRONCOS	23
BROWNS	20
RAIDERS	20
RAVENS	12
COWBOYS	27
REDSKINS	0
PANTHERS	20
FALCONS	17
PACKERS	38
CHARGERS	21
BENGALS	41
49ERS	38
SAINTS	45
GIANTS	7

Details, Pages 122, 85, 84

STAFF PHOTO BY MICHAEL SEAMANS

PICK OF THE LITTER: Patriots cornerback Tyrone Poole holds the football high as he and teammate Ty Law celebrate Poole's first of two second-half interceptions during yesterday's 27-13 victory over the Jacksonville Jaguars at Gillette Stadium.

THE QUINTESSENTIAL ESSENTIAL
The Ears Have It!
BEST OF BOSTON 2003
Diamond Earrings
Every Shape & Size
DePrisco
DIAMOND JEWELERS SINCE 1948
BOSTON JEWELERS EXCHANGE BUILDING · 333 WASHINGTON STREET, BOSTON, MA 617-227-3339
178 LINDEN PLAZA, WELLESLEY, MA 781-237-2700 · 32 WIANNO AVENUE, OSTERVILLE, MA 508-420-7400

A COORDINATED EFFORT

Bill Belichick's top lieutenants, Charlie Weis and Romeo Crennel, finally appear ripe for a rise to NFL head coaching positions

STAFF PHOTOS BY MATTHEW WEST AND MICHAEL SEAMANS (INSET RIGHT)

CALLING THE SHOTS: Patriots offensive coordinator Charlie Weis is the man behind the plan for head coach Bill Belichick — and the man behind quarterback Tom Brady during one of last week's workouts in the practice bubble.

STAFF PHOTOS BY MATTHEW WEST AND MICHAEL SEAMANS (INSET LEFT)

DIRECT APPROACH: Patriots defensive coordinator Romeo Crennel, the right-hand man in head coach Bill Belichick's two-gap scheme, shouts orders to defensive lineman Rick Lyle during practice last week.

By KAREN GUREGIAN

FOXBORO — Their names are being mentioned as potential candidates with every NFL coach firing or rumored firing. Their mugshots are included prominently in every future candidate lineup.

Pick a job opening across the league, and Romeo Crennel and Charlie Weis are likely to be found high on the list of candidates. Already, their faces have been flashed across the screens of NFL.com and are adorning sports pages and football magazines across the country every time an NFL coach gets canned.

Having learned and honed their craft under both Bill Parcells and Bill Belichick, having been a part of Super Bowl winning teams, having already helped the Patriots to an AFC East championship this season, both defensive coordinator Crennel and offensive coordinator Weis are seen as attractive catches.

Given the wealth of vacancies — openings already exist with the Falcons and Giants, with others projected down the road — Patriots players are well aware they could lose one, or both, of their top assistants in the offseason.

In fact, Giants general manager Ernie Accorsi let it be known that he planned to stay behind on the Giants' trip to Dallas to attend last night's Patriots-Jets game and "scout" Crennel and Weis.

"It's like teams around the league see what's going on here. And everyone wants to capture some of the magic," Pats quarterback Tom Brady said Thursday. "Obviously, they can't get Coach Belichick, so they'll try and take his lieutenants. There's no mystery. Those guys are great coaches. Charlie is certainly one of the top ones in the league. They'll be big shoes for someone to try and fill."

For the players, it's somewhat of a bittersweet situation. They would love to see Crennel and Weis advance in their careers, but at the same time, they hate the thought of losing them.

Helping hands

Brady is especially fond of Weis, and though [...]sition to do well. He's always prepared, and it does sound like at some point we'll lose him, unfortunately, from everything you hear. It'll be tough, because he's so capable.

"Especially, with the development and rapport we've had for three or four years. Any time you lose a coach that you respect so much, that would (expletive). But I think it's a goal of his. At some point it's everyone's goal to reach the top. There's no doubt he's capable. That's obvious."

Weis would like a top job, and in the past has made no secret of that desire — even expressing an interest in the University of Washington job in the offseason — but doesn't want that "sidebar" issue, as he put it, to get in the way of preparing his offense. Crennel pretty much offered the same response during an interview Thursday, but was a little more open about discussing the future.

"We're both honored to be considered for any job we may be considered for. But no one has contacted me. Everything right now is rumor and innuendo," Crennel said. "I'm just trying to do the best job I can."

Crennel, who is in his 23rd NFL season, seventh as a Patriots coach, does envision himself as a head coach. Some coordinators are happy being just that and don't want the added responsibility. Not Crennel. He definitely wants the opportunity to run the show.

"Yes, I do," he said. "I've put some time in in this business. I've gained some experience in this business. I feel like I can do the job, and would like the opportunity to do the job. I think everybody's goal is to try and be at the top of their profession, and it's one of mine."

The players Crennel directs and guides through all of his complex defensive schemes sound more like cheerleaders when talking about Crennel in regard to all the expected coaching vacancies. Many of them last week openly lobbied and campaigned for Crennel to get consideration down the road.

The only thing missing from the discussion were pompoms.

"Romeo is a very knowledgeable guy. He's really into it. He lives and breathes football. He loves it. A guy like that really deserves an opportunity to be a head coach somewhere," remarked safety Rodney Harrison, who's in the midst of his first season under Crennel. "He pays the price. He's a very knowledgeable guy. He studies hard. He really bleeds it. I believe he's well-deserving of consideration."

Romeo out front

Of the two coordinators, Crennel has been getting a bit more attention in terms of being a slam-dunk for a job in the 2004 season. Sports Illustrated's Peter King indicated to WEEI that one of his sources guaranteed Crennel would land one of the coaching vacancies. NFL.com, meanwhile, had Crennel's picture front and center in a story about future candidates.

One of the reasons for Crennel's added exposure stems from the fact his defense has been nearly unpenetrable for much of the season. It hadn't allowed a home-field touchdown in what amounted to five games before Jacksonville scored one with 3:20 left in last week's 27-13 Patriots win at Gillette Stadium.

Many players believe he hasn't gotten nearly enough credit for their success over the years.

"He's the glue that keeps the defense together," cornerback Ty Law remarked. "Everyone talks about Coach Belichick every time they mention our defense. But, Belichick isn't in our meetings. I think (Crennel) should get more credit for what's going on back there. He's a great coach, he's paid his dues.

"To be honest with you, I'd hate to see him leave, but I think he deserves a shot at being a head coach because he knows how to bring the team together, he knows how to put people in the right situations, he knows what to call in certain situations. He's been second fiddle for a long time. He's got his credit among the players, but he's coached a lot longer than other guys who've gotten opportunities. He's coached on Super Bowl champion teams. I just think he should get his just due."

Opposite tacks

It's interesting Weis and Crennel are somewhat opposite in their approach to coaching. Weis is said to be tough and hard-nosed, much like Parcells. Crennel is a kinder, gentler version by most accounts. Crennel considers himself more a teacher than anything else. And judging by how well the players have grasped the defense, and how well they execute his game plan, he's a very good teacher.

"I would say he's a player's coach, and that's the best type of coach a player can have," cornerback Tyrone Poole said. "He cares. He's understanding of his players needs, their feelings, and how the game is played from a players' standpoint. I would be glad to see him go out and become a head coach. I think he'd be a great head coach. I'd play for him any day."

Under the new NFL guidelines, Weis and Crennel will have a small window of opportunity to interview during the postseason. Should the Pats earn a first-round bye, the window will be Dec. 28-Jan. 2. Should the Pats play a wild card game, it will be Jan. 4-9. Beyond that, talks will be prohibited until after the Pats' playoff run ends.

"If Mr. (Robert) Kraft and Bill are asked, and they tell me it's OK, then I will interview," Weis told the Herald last week. "If they're not asked or they say it's not OK, then I won't. They're the bosses and I'll go with what they tell me."

Unkind cut for Weis

Weis underwent gastric bypass surgery two years ago and subsequent complications nearly cost him his life. Today, he is almost fully recovered save for a "drop foot" condition that has forced him to wear a brace.

There are those who think Weis had the surgery to enhance his chances at winning a head job. But Weis maintains that wasn't the case.

"I know why I did it, because I probably would have dropped dead if I didn't," said Weis, who insists it was done to provide security for his wife and kids. "When you're well over 300 pounds for a long amount of time, you're a walking heart attack. It's helped in every perspective. And I can tell you I feel a lot better."

The players he coaches on offense with are also quick to endorse him for a head job. The Pats offense, (18th in the NFL heading into last night's game), while not overwhelming, has scored enough points despite a lackluster running game, and an injury-riddled receiving corps.

"Guys who get hired usually come from winning programs," said Pats guard Joe Andruzzi. "A guy like Charlie, he's been in the league for a while. He understands the system, he knows the NFL. I think he'd be a great head coach."

And a great loss for the Pats?

"Yeah, because we know what to expect from

The Weis file

NAME — Charlie Weis
BORN — March 30, 1956, Trenton, N.J.
TITLE — Offensive coordinator
COLLEGE — Earned a bachelor's degree in communications and education at Notre Dame. Earned his master's degree in education at South Carloina
COACHING EXPERIENCE — 25 years
NFL EXPERIENCE — 14 years
TENURE WITH PATRIOTS — 8 years
PRO HIGHLIGHTS — His contributions have helped produce two Super Bowl championships (New York and New England), three conference titles and four division titles.
AMATEUR HIGHLIGHTS — Assistant at the University of Carolina for four seasons ... Head coach at Franklin Township (N.J.) High in 1989. That year, he directed them to the state championship ... Also coached at Boonton High and Morristown High in New Jersey.
PERSONAL — Charlie and his wife Maura have two children, Charles Joseph and Hannah Margaret.

COACHING HISTORY

Yr.	Team	Position
1979	Boonton (N.J.) High	Assistant coach
1980-84	Morristown (N.J.) High	Assistant coach
1985-88	South Carolina	Assistant coach
1989	Franklin Township High	Head coach
1990	New York Giants	Defensive assistant
1991-92	New York Giants	Running backs coach
1993-94	PATRIOTS	Tight ends coach
1995	PATRIOTS	Running backs coach
1996	PATRIOTS	Wide receivers coach
1997	New York Jets	Wide receivers coach
1998	New York Jets	Off. coordinator/FBs
1999	New York Jets	Off. coordinator/RBs
2000	PATRIOTS	Off. coordinator/RBs
[illegible]	PATRIOTS	Off. coordinator/RBs
[illegible]	[illegible]	Off. coordinator/QBs
[illegible]	[illegible]	Offensive coordinator

The Crennel file

NAME — Romeo Crennel
BORN — June 18, 1947, Lynchburg, Va
TITLE — Defensive coordinator/Defensive line coach
COLLEGE — Earned a bachelor's degree in physical education from Western Kentucky. Also earned a master's degree there.
COACHING EXPERIENCE — 34 years
NFL EXPERIENCE — 23 years
TENURE WITH PATRIOTS — 7 years
PRO HIGHLIGHTS — As an assistant, has helped earn three Super Bowl titles (two in New York, one in New England), four conference titles and six division titles.
AMATEUR HIGHLIGHTS — Served as defensive assistant at four different colleges including line coach at Texas Tech under defensive coordinator Bill Parcells.
PLAYING HISTORY — Four-year starter (1966-69) as a defensive lineman at Western Kentucky. Was headed for all-conference honors before switching from defensive lineman to offensive tackle to help fill in for an injured player. Earned team MVP honors that season.
PERSONAL — Romeo and his wife Rosemary have three daughters, Lisa, Tiffany, and Kristen. His brother Carl, played linebacker for the CFL's Hamilton Tiger Cats.

COACHING HISTORY

Yr.	Team	Position
1970	Western Kentucky	Graduate assistant
1971-74	Western Kentucky	Defensive line
1975-77	Texas Tech	Defensive assistant
1978-79	Mississippi	Defensive ends
1980	Georgia Tech	Defensive line
1981-82	New York Giants	Special teams/defense
1983-89	New York Giants	Special teams
1990-92	New York Giants	Defensive line
1993-96	PATRIOTS	Defensive line
1997-99	New York Jets	Defensive line
2000	Cleveland Browns	Def. coord. [illegible]
2001	PATRIOTS	[illegible]
2002-0[illegible]	[illegible]	[illegible]

Sports

Upstart Panthers beat up on Eagles
Carolina makes it to first Super Bowl
Page 100

Houston, we have contact

PATS LAND SUPER BOWL BERTH BY CORRALLING MANNING, COLTS
Coverage, Pages 127-102

STAFF PHOTO BY MICHAEL SEAMANS

BACKLASH: Patriots defensive lineman Jarvis Green sacks Colts quarterback Peyton Manning during yesterday's 24-14 victory in the AFC Championship Game in Foxboro.

1 Month Free!
Must be 18 Years or older. New Members Only.
Team Super Fitness Centers Inc.
FREE Personal Training for All Members
www.teamsuperfitness.com
Quincy, MA • 617-770-1115 Malden, MA • 781-324-6000 Watertown, MA • 617-923-4441 Danvers, MA • 978-777-3666
ANC
AMERICAN NUTRITION CENTER
738 Broadway, EVERETT
617-394-0678
$25.99
OU-TORN
$9.99
www.anceverett.com
20-50% OFF EVERYDAY

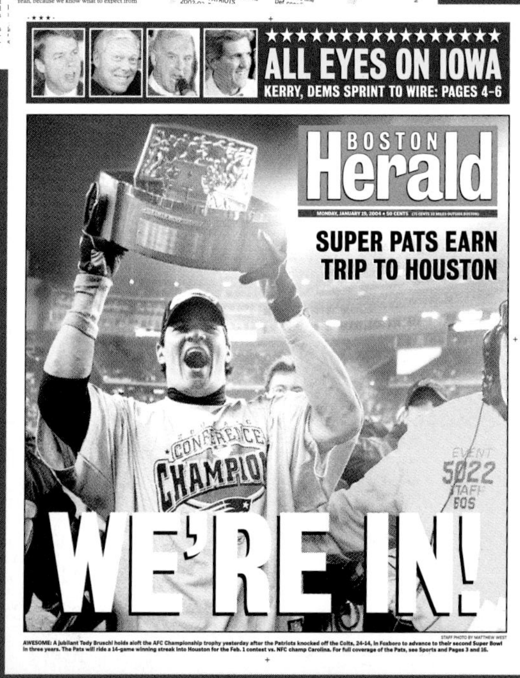
ALL EYES ON IOWA
KERRY, DEMS SPRINT TO WIRE: PAGES 4-6

BOSTON Herald
MONDAY, JANUARY 19, 2004 • 50 CENTS

SUPER PATS EARN TRIP TO HOUSTON

WE'RE IN!

STAFF PHOTO BY MATTHEW WEST

AWESOME: A jubilant Tedy Bruschi holds aloft the AFC Championship trophy yesterday after the Patriots knocked off the Colts, 24-14, in Foxboro to advance to their second Super Bowl in three years. The Pats will ride a 14-game winning streak into Houston for the Feb. 1 contest vs. NFC champ Carolina. For full coverage of the Pats, see Sports and Pages 3 and 16.

TIME TO BOUNCE BACK
Patriots start camp thinking redemption

BY MICHAEL FELGER, BOSTON HERALD

I've been knocked down so many times, counted out six, seven, eight, nine, written off like some bad deal. If you're breathing, you know how it feels. Call it karma, call it luck. Me, I just don't give a . . . Bounce, bounce, nothing's going to keep me down. Bounce, bounce. I play hard. I play to win. Count me out. Count me in. I'll be bouncing back again.

—From Jon Bon Jovi's "Bounce"

Those words echoed through Gillette Stadium as F.O.B.B (friend of Bill Belichick) Jon Bon Jovi sang his song of perserverance and defiance to a sold-out crowd. The song is dedicated to Belichick on the album's CD cover (check it out).

It's a fitting sentiment as Belichick heads into his fourth training camp as Patriots head coach. Smarting from a disappointing 2002 season in which the Pats failed to validate their 2001 NFL championship by missing the playoffs, Belichick and his staff have seen several changes come to the team, not the least of which is a renewed sense of urgency.

"When I got here I could sense that immediately," said prize free agent linebacker Rosevelt Colvin from the Pats' locker room yesterday. "There was a real disappointment here. But a confidence, too, in what the team can do. This team isn't going to take anything for granted. Everyone is on the same page."

Colvin represents one of the Pats' most significant changes this year—the decision to dip into big-money free agency. Most of that money was spent on the defense; Colvin will be joined by former Pro Bowl safety Rodney Harrison and veteran cornerback Tyrone Poole.

Speed was also a priority on the personnel front, as the Pats drafted a pair of players in the second round—cornerback Eugene Wilson and receiver Bethel Johnson—who will immediately become two of the fastest players on the team. Colvin, Poole and free agent receiver Dedric Ward will also improve the team's speed.

There have been substantive schematic changes as well, particularly on defense, where Belichick was horrified with a unit that finished 31st in the league against the run, 24th on third downs and 30th in the red zone. Colvin will be a featured player in the new 3-4 base scheme, with an emphasis on getting to the quarterback.

"I can already tell that what Belichick does so well is mix it up," said Colvin, who had 21 sacks the past two years as a member of the Bears. "I can play as a linebacker or end, just like about six other guys on this defense. I blitzed over [60 percent] of the time in Chicago, so hopefully they'll be putting me in position to make plays here. That's all you can ask for."

OPPOSITE: Kevin Faulk (left) and Antowain Smith work out during practice at training camp. (George Martell/Boston Herald)

New linebacker Roosevelt Colvin wipes sweat from his brow toward the end of practice.
(Michael Seamans/Boston Herald)

Another huge change is the venue. The Pats will be training in Foxboro after years at Bryant College in Smithfield, R.I.

Logistically, the biggest concern many players have is with—get this—their nap time. At Bryant, the players were forced to stay in cramped, dingy dorm rooms. But at least those living quarters were a short walk from the dining hall, giving the players ample opportunity to head back to their rooms, shut the door and recharge their batteries.

This year, the entire team will be housed at a hotel three miles away from the stadium. The rooms will be an upgrade over Bryant, but the distance between bed and field will present some problems.

The number of two-a-day practices will be cut dramatically, with only six currently scheduled. But these are not normal double sessions. Belichick has altered the schedule so the first practice comes before the sun gets brutal in the morning (9-11 a.m.) and after it blazes in the afternoon (6-8 p.m.). There will be no double sessions on consecutive days.

The moves were made in part to account for heat-related issues that the NFL is suddenly taking seriously. But Belichick also instituted them to make the commute between the hotel and the stadium more palatable.

As for nap time, the team will have shuttle buses going back and forth during the day and will allow players to drive their own cars back to the hotel to hit the sack. The Pats have also set aside one room in the stadium with bunks for players who want to stay on site, as well as a game room with ping-pong tables and video games for those wishing for another diversion.

So all systems are in place and the changes have been made. Now Belichick hopes to see the bounce.

Quarterbacks (left to right) Damon Huard, Tom Brady and Rohan Davey throw to receivers during training camp prac-

NEW ENGLAND 0

GAME ONE

BUFFALO 31

BRADY FAILS FIRST TEST
Throws four interceptions in loss to Bills

BY MICHAEL GEE, BOSTON HERALD

Tom Brady sat on the Patriots' bench and stared straight ahead. The action on the field was an ugly sight, but it sure beat gazing at the scoreboard.

That read Buffalo 31, New England 0. Brady was on the sidelines because he'd been yanked for garbage time to put a merciful end to the worst game of the Pats' quarterback's still-brief pro career.

No doubt about it. Buffalo coach Gregg Williams is inside Brady's head. The Bills' defense tormented Brady, transforming him into a one-man NFL Films blooper reel.

"Oh, sure," Brady said when asked if he was embarrassed. "That's not the way I should play. We have NO chance when that happens."

Few teams win when their quarterback passes for just 123 yards, completing 14-of-29 attempts. Fewer still succeed if he throws four interceptions and has one returned for a touchdown.

Brady hit that dismal trifecta on the nose, a "performance" good for a quarterback rating of 20.4.

"A screen pass for an interception, another one a defensive lineman caught it, another one bounced off a helmet," a mystified Brady said. "That sort of stuff hasn't happened to us."

Against a frenzied Bills defense, catastrophe became Brady's constant companion.

Aside from a brilliant play off a deflection by Buffalo corner Nate Clements, Brady's picks were unforced errors of an amateurish nature. Sam Adams at 335 pounds is an obstacle a quarterback should be able to avoid with a thrown ball. Brady hit Adams amidships with a toss the Bills tackle returned 37 yards for a tragicomic touchdown.

When Brady misfires, the Patriots' offense simply vanishes. In the first quarter, New England ran all of three plays. Brady didn't complete a pass to a wide receiver until the third quarter, and he finished the first half with an amazing QB rating of 5.3. The Pats were lucky zero is the lowest score the rules allow.

No team could survive a game from its QB like the one Brady had. But the Pats can't afford Brady to even be mediocre. If he's not one of the most efficient and productive passers in the league, they can't score enough to win.

Kevin Faulk had a nice game yesterday, but Earl Campbell he ain't. As a group, the Pats' skill people aren't track stars. Their attack depends on precision, the ingredient Brady is supposed to supply.

So it's worrisome for New England to note that while extreme, Brady's performance was not out of line with some of the games he had down the stretch in 2002. Let's be blunt. The Pats' indispensable hero is in a slump.

And maybe Gregg Williams has something to do with it after all. Because Brady's dropoff began the last time these two clubs met, 10 months ago this very day at Gillette Stadium.

Tom Brady is sacked by No. 95 Sam Adams in the first quarter.
(Michael Seamans/Boston Herald)

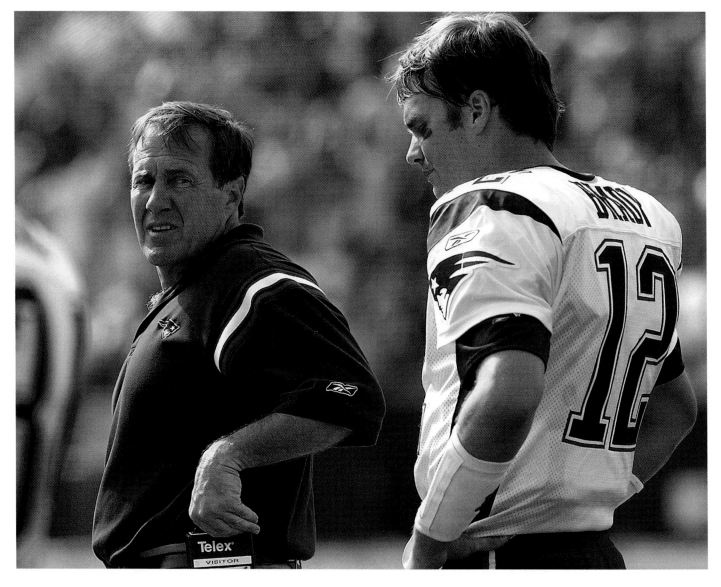

Head coach Bill Belichick looks back at a dejected Tom Brady after Brady threw his fourth interception of the game. (Michael Seamans/Boston Herald)

In the second half of the Pats' 27-17 win, Brady went 4-for-11 for 22 yards. Since then, he hasn't had a game with more TD passes than interceptions. Overall, in what's now 4 1/2 straight games, Brady is 72-of-150 for 623 yards, two touchdowns and seven interceptions.

That's not a Tiger Woods slump. That's a David Duval slump. Not coincidentally, the Pats are 1-3 in Brady's last four games, their only win stemming from the Dolphins' gag job in the 2002 finale.

Every NFL team, even the eventual Super Bowl champ, plays one flat-out stinkeroo each season. Getting that disaster out of the way early may not cause the Pats too much harm this year.

"We've got to get better, and I think we will get better," Brady said.

Quarterback, heal thyself. If Brady can't regain the form he had in the first part of last season, the Pats won't get better enough to make the playoffs.

If Brady's woes continue, the Pats won't have to go another 10 years between shutout losses. Seven days might do it.

"We've got to get better, and I think we will get better."

—Patriots QB Tom Brady

Former Patriot Lawyer Milloy closes in on Tom Brady for a second-quarter sack. (Michael Seamans/Boston Herald)

	1st	2nd	3rd	4th	Final
New England	0	0	0	0	0
Buffalo	7	14	0	10	31

SCORING SUMMARY

Qtr	Team	Play		Time
1	Bills	TD	Henry 1-yd. run (Lindell kick)	9:58
2	Bills	TD	Moore 7-yd. pass from Bledsoe (Lindell kick)	13:22
2	Bills	TD	Adams 37-yd. interception return (Lindell kick)	10:14
4	Bills	TD	Henry 9-yd. run (Lindell kick)	13:21
4	Bills	FG	Lindell 44-yd.	4:16

OFFENSE

PATRIOTS

PASSING	COMP	ATT	YDS	TD	INT
Brady	14	29	123	0	4
Davey	3	6	31	0	0

RECEIVING	REC	YDS	TD
Patten	2	48	0
Faulk	4	25	0
B. Johnson	2	25	0
Centers	4	18	0
Smith	1	12	0
T. Brown	1	10	0
Branch	1	8	0
Fauria	1	7	0
Graham	1	1	0

RUSHING	ATT	YDS	TD
Faulk	10	62	0
Centers	5	36	0
Smith	6	7	0

BILLS

PASSING	COMP	ATT	YDS	TD	INT
Bledsoe	17	28	230	1	1

RECEIVING	REC	YDS	TD
Moulds	4	81	0
Shaw	3	51	0
Henry	3	37	0
Morris	2	25	0
Campbell	3	24	0
Moore	1	7	1
Reed	1	5	0

RUSHING	ATT	YDS	TD
Henry	28	86	2
Morris	2	14	0
Burns	2	4	0
Bledsoe	1	0	0

ECSTASY AND AGONY: Buffalo QB Drew
Bledsoe pumps his fists after a touchdown pass
in the second quarter as Richard Seymour reacts.
(Michael Seamans/Boston Herald)

NEW ENGLAND 31

GAME TWO

PHILADELPHIA 10

PATS GET IT TOGETHER
Regain emotional edge in 31-10 rout of Eagles

BY MICHAEL FELGER, BOSTON HERALD

If there is hatred in the Patriots' locker room, then there was plenty of love between the lines this night.

Putting 12 days of controversy and acrimony behind them, the Patriots rebounded to put their season back on track against the Philadelphia Eagles at Lincoln Financial Field. The game may have been more of a statement on the Eagles' ineptitude than the Patriots' excellence, but it all added up to the same thing: an improbable 31-10 blowout victory when the Pats needed it the most.

Veteran safety Rodney Harrison, who is fast becoming a team leader in the mold of the Pats' former strong safety (what's his name?) believed attitude was the biggest factor. He was asked the difference between Game Two's Patriots team and the one that was blown out in Buffalo.

"Emotion," said Harrison, who was all over the field, knocking down four passes and recording three tackles. "You have to have it in this league. You can't just go out there and think it's all going to be there. You have to match intensity. And we did that. We played how the Patriots should play."

Was there a turning point when the Pats regained that emotion?

"Yeah, on Wednesday," said Harrison, "when Coach [Bill Belichick] came into our meeting and basically gave it to us. He told us we have to match their intensity."

If the players were listening to Belichick, that certainly ran counter to what ESPN analyst Tom Jackson said on his pregame show, that the Patriots "hate their coach."

The Patriots' organization heard the comment loud and clear. Owner Bob Kraft was said to be furious about it. Another high-ranking team official, with sarcasm dripping from his voice, added: "Appears to be real accurate, huh?"

"I don't want to speak for Coach," Harrison said. "But I know this was a huge game for him. With all that stuff that went on last week, we needed this. He needed this."

Added Belichick: "I'm really proud of the way we came together in all three areas. Our guys showed a lot of toughness. We kept our poise in a couple of tough situations and made some plays."

For the first time all year, the Patriots came out from the pregame tunnel as a team, eschewing individual introductions. Then they proceeded to put together a complete team game.

OPPOSITE: No. 54 Tedy Bruschi & Co. celebrate his fourth-quarter sack of Philadelphia's Donovan McNabb. (Matthew West/Boston Herald)

Willie McGinest drags No. 22 Duce Staley after his fourth-quarter interception.
(Matthew West/Boston Herald)

The Eagles were just the opposite, and the numbers tell the story. They had six turnovers. They converted just 3-of-14 third downs. And quarterback Donovan McNabb had his worst game in recent memory, completing just 18-of-46 passes for 186 yards while compiling a hideous rating of 33.4.

The Patriots converted most of the Eagles' miscues into points. A McNabb fumble in the second quarter led to an 8-yard scoring pass from Tom Brady to Christian Fauria, and a muffed punt by Brian Westbrook led to a 5-yard hookup with Fauria later in the quarter.

The Pats' third score came on a pretty 26-yard pass from Brady to Deion Branch on a post pattern in the third quarter. From there, the Pats tried (mostly unsuccessfully) to run the clock while McNabb and the Eagles tried in vain to move the ball through the air. Tedy Bruschi put the icing on the cake with an 18-yard interception return for a touchdown late in the fourth quarter.

Each time the Eagles' offense came off the field, the boos grew louder. This will be a bad week to be an Eagle, but a good week if you're a talk show host in Philadelphia. The Eagles have a bye this weekend.

"We need to get back on track," said Eagles coach Andy Reid.

The Pats' offense reverted to the five-wide, empty-nest scheme that has brought it success in the past. Brady was the beneficiary, as he completed 30-of-44 attempts for 255 yards and three touchdowns.

On defense, the Pats were far quicker to the ball than they were a week ago in Buffalo. The results were obvious.

"We needed that," said defensive end Bobby Hamilton. "We can't control what's going on upstairs. We can only control how we play as a team. And we did that today. We fought hard and came together."

"It's not going to be easy," said linebacker Mike Vrabel. "You have guys go down and you have to have others step up. That's what we did today and that's what we have to keep doing."

"It's not going to be easy. You have guys go down and you have to have others step up. That's what we did today and that's what we have to keep doing."

—Patriots linebacker Mike Vrabel

Mike Vrabel takes down Eagles QB Donovan McNabb in the third. (Matthew West/Boston Herald)

	1st	2nd	3rd	4th	Final
New England	3	14	7	7	31
Philadelphia	0	7	0	3	10

SCORING SUMMARY

Qtr	Team	Play		Time
1	Patriots	FG	Vinatieri 27-yd.	1:10
2	Eagles	TD	Staley 2-yd. run (Akers kick)	14:00
2	Patriots	TD	Fauria 8-yd. pass from Brady (Vinatieri kick)	7:59
2	Patriots	TD	Fauria 5-yd. pass from Brady (Vinatieri kick)	2:09
3	Patriots	TD	Branch 26-yd. pass from Brady (Vinatieri kick)	7:02
4	Eagles	FG	Akers 57-yd.	10:48
4	Patriots	TD	Bruschi 18-yd. interception return (Vinatieri kick)	5:02

OFFENSE

PATRIOTS

PASSING	COMP	ATT	YDS	TD	INT
Brady	30	44	255	3	0

RECEIVING	REC	YDS	TD
Branch	6	89	1
Faulk	4	59	0
T. Brown	7	43	0
B. Johnson	2	21	0
Fauria	3	19	2
Centers	2	12	0
Patten	2	4	0
Graham	1	3	0
McCrary	1	3	0
Smith	2	2	0

RUSHING	ATT	YDS	TD
Smith	12	25	0
Faulk	7	23	0
Brady	6	7	0
Centers	3	7	0
McCrary	1	0	0
Walter	1	0	0

EAGLES

PASSING	COMP	ATT	YDS	TD	INT
McNabb	18	46	186	0	2
Detmer	2	2	25	0	0

RECEIVING	REC	YDS	TD
Thrash	6	80	0
Lewis	3	36	0
Pinkston	3	35	0
Buckhalter	1	21	0
Mitchell	3	16	0
Staley	3	16	0
Westbrook	1	7	0

RUSHING	ATT	YDS	TD
McNabb	6	53	0
Westbrook	6	29	0
Staley	5	17	1

Wide receiver No. 83 Deion Branch celebrates his touchdown catch in the third quarter, which put the Pats up 23-7, much to the chagrin of No. 26 Lito Sheppard. (Matthew West/Boston Herald)

TY LAW

CAN'T LOSE WITH TY

BY MICHAEL GEE, BOSTON HERALD

There's a tendency to take Ty Law for granted. Try to fight it.

The veteran cornerback is starting his ninth year with the Patriots. He has started every game he's been healthy enough to suit up for since the 1996 season (his second) began. He's made the Pro Bowl three times, including back-to-back appearances the last two seasons.

He's a fixture, a given.

It's a simple deal. Pencil Law in at left cornerback and assume the best. Whatever problems the Patriots' defense might have in 2003, Law's not going to be one of them. His performance will range from very good to superior.

It had better.

New England's secondary is in a state of mandatory flux. With the release of safety Lawyer Milloy. Law is the only returning starter. He has lost his fellow Pro Bowler (Milloy), his familiar partner at corner (Otis Smith) and safety Tebucky Jones.

The Patriots have brought in rookies Eugene Wilson and Asante Samuel, and free agent Tyrone Poole, to handle the chores at right corner.

Veterans HATE it when another vet is let go. That sentiment escalates exponentially when it's a guy at their own position, not to mention one with whom they shared a Super Bowl championship.

Law was so upset when Smith was cut he refused all comment, later explaining he didn't want to say something he'd regret. But even before Smith's departure, Law kept a low profile in training camp.

Perhaps that's because Law's contract, earning him more than $6 million a season, makes him one of the highest-paid players in the NFL at a position where teams have traditionally looked to save money long before the advent of the salary cap. Law has so far refused to renegotiate his deal, something that led directly to Milloy's release. Some have even speculated Wilson and Samuel were drafted precisely to remind Law that in pro football, every player is an expendable commodity.

But not every player is an expendable commodity at all times. A corner coming off a Pro Bowl season, the team leader in interceptions, Law's job remains secure because the rest of the Pats' organization wants theirs to stay the same.

Nine-year veteran Ty Law is a
fixture on the Patriots' roster.
(Kuni Takahashi/Boston Herald)

NEW YORK JETS 16

GAME THREE

NEW ENGLAND 23

PAIN IS SECONDARY CONCERN
Samuel steps up to save wounded Pats

BY HOWARD BRYANT, BOSTON HERALD

Up until Asante Samuel made the play of the day, the Patriots not only didn't know where their next big play was going to come from, but if there would be anyone left to make one in the first place.

They eventually beat the Jets, 23-16, but these are starting to look like desperate times for the Patriots. Bill Belichick and his charges already knew before the victory that game-changing plays wouldn't be coming from Rosevelt Colvin, who is gone for the season with a fractured hip, or Ted Johnson, out with a broken foot until somewhere around Halloween. During the game, Belichick found he couldn't look to Ted Washington—who fractured his leg during the first half, or Ty Law, David Patten or Mike Vrabel, all of whom left the game wounded.

By the time the game ended, three starters—Vrabel, Patten and Washington—were out of the lineup, while Law limped and Tom Brady smiled while his right elbow sizzled with pain.

While the Patriots found themselves adding up the number of fallen big names, an inferior Jets team stayed just close enough to make them—and the 68,436 in the seats—wonder if this afternoon was going to end up badly. For most of the game, one score separated the two clubs when the game really shouldn't have been close at all.

And with the Patriots only up 16-9, Belichick couldn't be blamed for wondering not only how he was going to win the game, but just how his Patriots were going to fulfill his grand vision for this season with no fewer than five starters already out.

With Law on the sideline with a twisted ankle, Samuel gave the coach an answer. On the first play of the final period, he tipped and then snatched a Vinny Testaverde pass intended for Wayne Chrebet at the Patriots' 45-yard line on third-and-5, racing 55 yards for a touchdown and a 23-9 lead.

That's what life is for these Pats, a team excited about snapping a five-game home losing streak to the Jets, but—outside of Samuel's big moment—one that cannot be overly enthusiastic about the way it played. Nor can it be too comforting to rely on rookies to turn big games around.

"It's a great feeling," Samuel said. "When someone gets hurt, you have to step up and do something. That's the chance you want. I saw the man-to-man coverage, he made his break, and I went for the ball."

It is a high-risk, high-reward kind of investment, but the Patriots may well depend on rookies like Samuel

OPPOSITE: Cornerback Ty Law couldn't pull in a second-quarter interception and was forced to leave the game with a twisted ankle. (Michael Seamans/Boston Herald)

Roman Phifer wrestles Jets running back Curtis Martin to the ground in the third quarter.
(Matthew West/Boston Herald)

and Eugene Wilson to turn mediocre performances into successful ones.

"I think Asante has got great feet and he is very savvy," Brady said. "He's just a smart player, knows the concept of the routes. I know that route he intercepted. We had a similar route that we ran this week. He does a great job of reading what the routes are looking like."

Rodney Harrison, the veteran safety, said the boom-or-bust nature of rookie life isn't something the Patriots can afford, but seasons can turn on the emergence of a new, unexpected force.

"Asante's a cocky player, and I like that. He knows he can play," Harrison said. "The key for him is going to be consistency, of not being too high during games like this, and not getting too low when you have bad ones. When you get too high around here you get knocked out of the clouds very quickly."

"I think Asante has got great feet and he is very savvy."

—Patriots QB Tom Brady

Tyrone Poole goes airborne to break up a long pass intended for No. 81 Curtis Conway. (Matthew West/Boston Herald)

	1st	2nd	3rd	4th	Final
New York Jets	3	3	3	7	16
New England	3	3	10	7	23

SCORING SUMMARY

Qtr	Team	Play	Time
1	Jets	FG	Brien 41-yd.	11:45
1	Patriots	FG	Vinatieri 24-yd.	5:58
2	Patriots	FG	Vinatieri 22-yd.	14:50
2	Jets	FG	Brien 39-yd.	6:33
3	Patriots	FG	Vinatieri 47-yd.	10:10
3	Jets	FG	Brien 30-yd.	5:37
3	Patriots	TD	Brady 1-yd. run (Vinatieri kick)	2:08
4	Patriots	TD	Samuel 55-yd. interception return (Vinatieri kick)	14:49
4	Jets	TD	Chrebet 29-yd. pass from Testaverde (Brien kick)	12:53

OFFENSE

JETS

PASSING	COMP	ATT	YDS	TD	INT
Testaverde	25	43	264	1	1
Stryzinski	0	1	0	0	0

RECEIVING	REC	YDS	TD
Conway	5	70	0
Chrebet	4	55	1
Sowell	5	36	0
Martin	4	34	0
Becht	3	30	0
Moss	1	17	0
Jordan	1	14	0
Baker	2	8	0

RUSHING	ATT	YDS	TD
Martin	15	53	0
Testaverde	1	7	0
Jordan	1	5	0

PATRIOTS

PASSING	COMP	ATT	YDS	TD	INT
Brady	15	25	181	0	0
Faulk	0	1	0	0	0

RECEIVING	REC	YDS	TD
Fauria	3	49	0
Graham	2	37	0
Branch	2	25	0
Centers	4	22	0
Patten	1	20	0
T. Brown	1	16	0
Faulk	2	12	0

RUSHING	ATT	YDS	TD
Faulk	17	79	0
Smith	13	55	0
T. Brown	1	7	0
Centers	2	7	0
Brady	3	-1	1

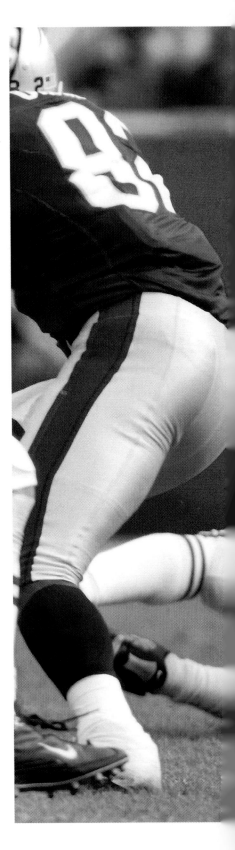

Kevin Faulk picks up yardage against
No. 57 Mo Lewis in second-half action.
(Matthew West/Boston Herald)

NEW ENGLAND 17

GAME FOUR

WASHINGTON 20

HEARTFELT LOSS
Patriots disconsolate despite noble effort

BY MICHAEL GEE, BOSTON HERALD

The Patriots were inconsolable.

Tom Brady sat staring at the blank wall behind his locker. Bill Belichick spoke in the terse, clipped phrases the coach uses in a futile attempt to hide sorrow.

On every Pats' face there was pain. When a Pat spoke, heartache dripped from every word. The final score—Redskins 20, Pats 17—was an insupportable burden to them all.

Any neutral observer with a soul wanted to give the Pats a good hug, to cheer them up, to issue the praise that was their due. They'd lost, but the Pats did far more honor to their cruel profession than did the guys who beat 'em.

The Pats were buried under an avalanche of miseries that would have caused Job to resign a head coaching position. Seven starters were missing due to injury. Recurrent turnovers had the team in a 20-3 third-quarter hole on the road.

Nobody would've blamed the Pats for submitting to a quick and quiet loss. Except themselves, that is, which made such an outcome impossible.

They don't always play well, and they don't always play smart, but my, do the Patriots always play.

The Pats rallied for two touchdowns. They turned the Redskins into a shell of themselves. By game's end, Washington was a shattered rabble whose only hope was the final whistle. No sane person could watch this contest without thinking better of the losers than the winners.

The Pats embodied almost all the good qualities of the term "professional athlete." They all gave two days' worth of flawed but honest work for a day's pay. Were I their coach or teammate, I'd be bursting with pride right now.

The Pats looked at themselves and saw nothing but a tremendous waste of said work. Theirs is the ultimate zero-sum universe. Players outgrow the moral victory concept in grade school.

Tackle Todd Light was one of two regulars on the five-man offensive line. That denuded outfit managed to get the Pats 106 yards rushing and surrendered just one sack in Brady's 39 pass plays.

Light didn't want to hear his gang had played its guts out. That was exactly why he was hurting.

"That's the thing," Light said. "You don't know how hard it is to come into an environment like that and you're surrounded by guys all giving 100 percent, and you lose. It's the toughest way to lose."

The Pats lost because of the errors that are the natural result of trying to do more than is possible or prudent. In a sense, their own courage was their opponent.

OPPOSITE: Kicker Adam Vinatieri (left) and holder Ken Walter walk off the field hanging their heads in disappointment after Vinatieri missed a key third-quarter field goal. (Matthew West/Boston Herald)

QB Tom Brady ponders his three interceptions en route to a three-point loss to the Redskins. (Matthew West/Boston Herald)

Brady threw some most inadvised passes that resulted in three interceptions and an incompletion on New England's final play. Offensive coordinator Charlie Weis razzled his own dazzle on two deadly occasions, a trick direct snap to Kevin Faulk, whose fumble set up Washington's first touchdown, and a failed draw play with Larry Centers on third-and-short on the Pats' next-to-last play.

That's what happens more often than not when a team knows it must sell out on every play to have a ghost of a chance. In the NFL, the perfect is indeed the enemy of the good.

The Pats know that, which is why Tedy Bruschi said he'd replay every single down of the game long into the night. The team knows something else, too: Moral victories aren't merely awful, they're dangerous.

"If we'd come away with a hard-fought win today it would have put us on a different level," Centers said.

Instead of believing they can surmount any adversity, the Pats look at the scoreboard and know they can't. In its current state, this team can sell out to the max against a mediocre foe begging to be beaten and still come up maddeningly short.

That's bitter self-knowledge to bear. And what devastated the Pats even more is that they also know that with the best will in the world, such maximum efforts become harder to duplicate if they don't pay off in results.

No team ever went on a moral victory streak. Pride and honor, alas, don't count toward earning a playoff share.

Running back Antowain Smith can't escape No.
56 LaVar Arrington in the third quarter.
(Matthew West/Boston Herald)

Tom Brady's second-quarter pass, intended for Deion Branch, is picked off by No. 26 Ifeanyi Ohalete. Brady threw two interceptions on the night. (Matthew West/Boston Herald)

	1st	2nd	3rd	4th	Final
New England	3	0	7	7	17
Washington	3	3	14	0	20

SCORING SUMMARY

Qtr	Team	Play		Time
1	Redskins	FG	Hall 38-yd.	9:42
1	Patriots	FG	Vinatieri 23-yd.	2:12
2	Redskins	FG	Hall 29-yd.	11:40
3	Redskins	TD	Betts 1-yd. run (Hall kick)	13:35
3	Redskins	TD	Cartwright 3-yd. run (Hall kick)	5:08
3	Patriots	TD	Givens 29-yd. pass from Brady (Vinatieri kick)	2:13
4	Patriots	TD	Centers 7-yd. pass from Brady (Vinatieri kick)	2:10

OFFENSE

PATRIOTS

PASSING	COMP	ATT	YDS	TD	INT
Brady	25	38	289	2	3

RECEIVING	REC	YDS	TD
T. Brown	7	60	0
Givens	4	57	1
Graham	3	54	0
Branch	3	38	0
Fauria	3	31	0
Centers	3	26	1
Smith	1	16	0
Faulk	1	7	0

RUSHING	ATT	YDS	TD
Smith	14	56	0
Centers	3	15	0
Faulk	10	12	0
Branch	1	11	0
T. Brown	1	10	0
Brady	1	2	0

REDSKINS

PASSING	COMP	ATT	YDS	TD	INT
Ramsey	10	22	147	0	0

RECEIVING	REC	YDS	TD
Coles	5	62	0
Morton	1	30	0
Canidate	1	25	0
Gardner	2	19	0
Cartwright	1	11	0

RUSHING	ATT	YDS	TD
Canidate	12	67	0
Betts	11	35	1
Ramsey	3	5	0
Johnson	1	4	0
Cartwright	1	3	1
Coles	1	2	0

RODNEY HARRISON

HARRISON COMES ON STRONG

BY MICHAEL FELGER, BOSTON HERALD

Remember all that talk about the Patriots' split-safety defense? Remember all of the declarations from the coaches about how there is no strong or free safety, just left and right? Remember all the time spent analyzing whether Lawyer Milloy and Rodney Harrison could coexist at the same position?

Uh, never mind.

"I'm the strong safety," Harrison said.

Harrison is now the one responsible for setting a physical tone in the Pats' secondary. The two-time Pro Bowler is the one who will line up the defense and call out the adjustments. He's the one who will creep up into the box to stuff the run. He's the one his teammates will look to as the last line of defense.

In other words, he'll be Lawyer Milloy.

"I feel like a rookie trying to come in and make the team," said Harrison, who is entering his 10th NFL season. "A lot of people know what I can do, but I'm looking forward to proving it to everyone again. I want to prove it to San Diego [which released him this off season]. I want to prove it to New England for bringing me here. I want to prove it to everyone in this locker room. I want to make a statement.

"I know people are going to be comparing me to Lawyer every step of the way. The stats, how we play, all of that. That's OK. It comes with the territory. But nothing is really changed. I'm going to go out and do what I've always done."

What Harrison has always done is dole out heavy hits over the middle of the field and provide valuable run support near the line of scrimmage.

Harrison admits the "most challenging part of the job" will be staying on top of all the schemes and making the right calls.

"I'm the one responsible for lining everyone up," Harrison said. "If I see a receiver out by himself, it's my job to get someone on him. Again, it's nothing I haven't done before, but it's a new system and new players. So that's something I'm definitely focusing on."

One thing is for certain: The view of Harrison as the aging veteran and Milloy as being in the prime of his career doesn't make sense, given their ages. Milloy is 29. Harrison is 30.

They are, in many ways, the same player. And they both have something to prove.

No. 37 Rodney Harrison steps
up to fill Lawyer Milloy's shoes.
(Michael Seamans/Boston Herald)

TENNESSEE 30

GAME FIVE

NEW ENGLAND 38

LAW AND ORDER RESTORED
Hobbled CB's pick locks up Pats' win

BY KEVIN MANNIX, BOSTON HERALD

The game was there to be lost. No question about it.

The Patriots had a 31-27 lead with a little more than three minutes remaining thanks to rookie Bethel Johnson's 71-yard kickoff return that set up Mike Cloud's 15-yard touchdown run. Still, there was no celebrating going on at Gillette Stadium.

Instead the fans were holding their breath, hoping that the Pats had one last stand in them. A four-point lead seemed hardly enough, not the way Steve McNair was airing it out and the way Tyrone Calico and Derrick Mason were torching the Patriots' secondary.

McNair was in the process of putting up a game's worth of offense in the final two quarters. During his second-half explosion, McNair completed 14-of-24 passes for 273 yards and a touchdown.

Across the line, the Pats were without Ty Law. The ankle injury that has bothered the cornerback since halftime of the Jets game two weeks ago flared up again early in the third quarter, sending him to the sidelines. When it didn't appear that the injury was going to get any better, the Pats' coaches adjusted the defense. Eugene Wilson moved from safety to cornerback and Antwan Harris was inserted at safety.

But as the Titans exploded, Law told coach Bill Belichick he was ready to make a comeback.

"When Ty came over to me and said he was ready to go back in the game, I wasn't really expecting that," Belichick said. "But Ty is a great competitor."

Four plays into the Titans' possession, Law anticipated a quick out-pass to Calico. Law jumped in front of the rookie to make the interception and didn't look too gimpy on the runback, either, as he returned it 65 yards for the decisive touchdown.

"You always anticipate something before every play," Law said. "I anticipated something quick to the sidelines on that play, so they could stop the clock. I took a gamble and it worked out for us. I couldn't play all the coverages we had, but the coaches gave me a chance to freelance."

Finally, the Pats and their fans could relax.

"They were playing so far off on the play and I knew he had a bad leg, so I thought I could get the ball in here," McNair said. "I didn't guess right on that. He broke on the ball and that was the ballgame."

Safety Rodney Harrison, who had a team-high 11 tackles, had a feeling the Titans would be going in Law's direction.

"When he came in, I looked at him and asked him if he was sure he was OK," Harrison said. "I saw

OPPOSITE: Tom Brady (top) celebrates No. 21 Michael Cloud's touchdown in the third quarter to put the Pats on top 20-16. (Kuni Takahashi/Boston Herald)

Antowain Smith rushes against Tennessee's Keith Bulluck. Smith finished the game with 16 carries for 80 yards and one touchdown. (Kuni Takahashi/Boston Herald)

him limping and I knew they'd be coming after him. He said, 'I'm ready. I have to do what I have to do.' When he came back to the sidelines after he scored, I went over to him and said, 'That's why you're the best.'

"In warmups, he told me he couldn't plant or push off the leg. But I knew the kind of soldier he is. But this whole team is like that. This is my first year here and seeing the way these guys step up through tough times shows the character these guys have. I'm learning about them and I'm glad to be a part of this."

Like Harrison, linebacker Tedy Bruschi viewed Law's grittiness as a symbol of the mentality of the entire team.

"That's what this team is about," Bruschi said. "From quarterback to kicker this is a tough team that grinds it out. We're missing guys and some of the guys on the field are dinged. Look at what Ty did. He was out for most of the game but came back in to make the play of the game.

"You could tell he was hurting, but when it came time to make a play, he forgot he was hurt. It looked like he was limping as he scored the touchdown, but that's the kind of thing that typifies the attitude of this team."

Fans congratulate Troy Brown after he scored on a pass from Brady for the first Patriots touchdown of the game. (Kuni Takahashi/Boston Herald)

	1st	2nd	3rd	4th	Final
Tennessee	6	7	3	14	30
New England	7	0	14	17	38

SCORING SUMMARY

Qtr	Team	Play		Time
1	Titans	FG	Hentrich 48-yd.	10:43
1	Titans	FG	Anderson 43-yd.	3:06
1	Patriots	TD	T. Brown 58-yd. pass from Brady (Vinatieri kick)	1:00
2	Titans	TD	McNair 1-yd. run (Anderson kick)	1:58
3	Patriots	TD	Smith 1-yd. run (Vinatieri kick)	9:25
3	Titans	FG	Anderson 33-yd.	5:31
3	Patriots	TD	Cloud 1-yd. run (Vinatieri kick)	0:58
4	Titans	FG	Anderson 37-yd.	13:19
4	Patriots	FG	Vinatieri 48-yd.	11:47
4	Titans	TD	McNair 1-yd. run (2-pt. conv. succeeds)	4:40
4	Patriots	TD	Cloud 15-yd. run (Vinatieri kick)	3:14
4	Patriots	TD	Law 65-yd. interception return (Vinatieri kick)	1:49
4	Titans	FG	Anderson 41-yd.	0:36

OFFENSE

TITANS

PASSING	COMP	ATT	YDS	TD	INT
McNair	23	45	391	0	1

RECEIVING	REC	YDS	TD
Mason	8	99	0
Calico	3	92	0
McCareins	2	72	0
Bennett	3	41	0
Holcombe	2	34	0
Kinney	2	26	0
Meier	1	14	0
George	2	13	0

RUSHING	ATT	YDS	TD
George	15	35	0
McNair	6	18	2
Mason	1	7	0
Brown	2	6	0
Holcombe	3	4	0

PATRIOTS

PASSING	COMP	ATT	YDS	TD	INT
Brady	17	31	219	1	0

RECEIVING	REC	YDS	TD
Branch	5	68	0
T. Brown	2	64	1
Fauria	2	33	0
Smith	3	23	0
Centers	4	18	0
Patten	1	13	0

RUSHING	ATT	YDS	TD
Smith	16	80	1
Cloud	7	73	2
Centers	1	6	0
Brady	3	2	0

Running back Michael Cloud dances into the end zone for his second and final touchdown to put the Pats up 30-27. (Kuni Takahashi/Boston Herald)

NEW YORK GIANTS 6

GAME SIX

NEW ENGLAND 17

SNAPPY MOVE BY BRADY
No-huddle play nixes Giants' challenge

BY GEORGE KIMBALL, BOSTON HERALD

A Patriots offense that had been all but nonexistent before halftime had finally started to move the ball. Tom Brady, who completed only one pass before intermission, had already completed three in a row when he rifled a 39-yard bomb to David Patten, who acrobatically pulled the ball in over Giants cornerback Will Peterson along the left sideline.

Patten stepped out of bounds at the Giants' 18, either just before, just after, or simultaneously with the reception.

The official on the spot ruled it a legal catch, but as the Fox telecast began flashing replays, Bill Belichick wasn't taking any chances. Alerted by assistants in the press box that it might be a close call, the Patriots' coach barked the order through his transmitter for his quarterback to get a play off—fast.

Brady, without huddling, shooed his troops up to the line, goosed center Dan Koppen, and plowed into the line.

The play gained 2 yards, but the Patriots didn't really care if they gained any. The idea was to stave off a replay challenge from the Giants, and as it turned out, Koppen's snap came a nanosecond ahead of Giants coach Jim Fassel's beanbag toss.

"We weren't sure whether [Patten] was in or not," said Belichick. "It was a long play, so we sacrificed a couple of yards there to make sure we got it run before they had a chance to review it. I don't know if he was in or not, but they said it was a real close play, and we have a term to trigger that. Tom did a good job hustling up to the line and got it off."

"We have some code words," Brady said. "I can't give you the word, but with a big play like that you don't even want to risk a challenge. We just wanted to get the snap off, and the guys did a good job getting up to the line, getting set, and running the play before they had a chance."

Was Patten in or out of bounds? We'll never know. When referee Bill Carollo ruled that Fassel's challenge came after the Patriots put the ball in play, the issue became forever moot, because it could no longer be reviewed.

Suffice it to say that two plays later, Mike Cloud banged over left guard for what proved to be the Patriots' only offensive touchdown of the day.

Brady couldn't remember ever having completed just one pass in 30 minutes of football, and it seemed even more unlikely that he'd ever gone 1-for-10 in the air and gone into the locker room at halftime with his team ahead.

OPPOSITE: Asante Samuel (left) celebrates with Eugene Wilson after blocking a pass intended for the Giants' Ike Hilliard. (Kuni Takahashi/Boston Herald)

A penalty on Richard Seymour (No. 93) can't spare Giants QB Kerry Collins the pain of a hard fourth-quarter hit by the big lineman. (Kuni Takahashi/Boston Herald)

"Most likely not," Brady said with a laugh. "That was not what we were looking for."

And it wasn't just Brady who was sputtering. By halftime the Patriots had been outgained, 199-29, in total yardage and had managed just one first down to the Giants' 12, yet led, 7-3, where it counted: on the scoreboard.

Given that the third quarter represented an almost complete turnaround from the first half, you might suppose that the Patriots' brain trust made radical adjustments at halftime, but you'd be wrong.

Belichick explained: "[Offensive coordinator] Charlie [Weis] and I talked about it at halftime, and Charlie told the team, 'We're not going to run any new

plays. In fact, some of the ones we were going to run in this game we're going to forget about. We'll just run the stuff that we know, but let's stop screwing it up.' And in the end we were able to get a couple of good drives in the third quarter and got enough points to win."

"They'd really dictated the tempo in the first half, but we went out and played better in the second," said Brady, who shook off his horrid first half to complete 7-of-11 for 105 in the second half. "Not that it was that great a second half, but it was better. We had a couple of scoring drives in the third quarter and we had a chance to put it away."

No. 58 Matt Chatham celebrates after returning a fumble 38 yards for the score.
(Kuni Takahashi/Boston Herald)

	1st	2nd	3rd	4th	Final
New York Giants	3	0	0	3	6
New England	7	0	10	0	17

SCORING SUMMARY

Qtr	Team	Play		Time
1	Patriots	TD	Chatham 38-yd. fumble return (Vinatieri kick)	12:24
1	Giants	FG	Conway 22-yd.	8:09
3	Patriots	FG	Vinatieri 28-yd.	10:39
3	Patriots	TD	Cloud 1-yd. run (Vinatieri kick)	4:22
4	Giants	FG	Conway 34-yd.	13:42

OFFENSE

GIANTS

PASSING	COMP	ATT	YDS	TD	INT
Collins	35	59	314	0	4

RECEIVING	REC	YDS	TD
Shockey	8	80	0
Hilliard	5	58	0
Rivers	4	49	0
Barber	8	48	0
Toomer	4	40	0
Carter	3	20	0
Finn	2	16	0
Shiancoe	1	3	0

RUSHING	ATT	YDS	TD
Barber	22	71	0
Collins	1	4	0
Joyce	1	0	0

PATRIOTS

PASSING	COMP	ATT	YDS	TD	INT
Brady	8	21	112	0	0

RECEIVING	REC	YDS	TD
Patten	3	55	0
Givens	1	21	0
B. Johnson	1	15	0
T. Brown	1	8	0
Fauria	1	7	0
Faulk	1	6	0

RUSHING	ATT	YDS	TD
Faulk	14	87	0
Cloud	9	23	1
T. Brown	2	12	0
Klecko	1	5	0
Patten	1	4	0
Brady	3	0	0
Centers	1	-2	0

Tom Brady (center) jumps on Michael Cloud (right) after Cloud's touchdown in the third quarter put the Pats up 11-3 against Giants. (Kuni Takahashi/Boston Herald)

ADAM VINATIERI

KICK START

BY JIM BAKER, BOSTON HERALD

Where would the Patriots be without the dead-on accuracy of place kicker Adam Vinatieri? Patriots fans are happily accustomed to counting on Vinatieri, but both coach Bill Belichick and center/guard Damien Woody say they're not taking him for granted.

"Adam gives me peace of mind," said Belichick, who's grateful because his team's injury-wracked state has otherwise brought turbulence. "He's better than sleeping pills. For consistency, I'd put him up there with anyone. With the game on the line, that's the guy I want out there."

Last season, he made 27-of-30 to lead the NFL in field goal percentage and earn his first Pro Bowl appearance.

Vinatieri totaled 805 points in his first seven seasons after going undrafted and signing as a free agent in 1996.

He's best known for the clutch 45-yard kick in heavy snow to force overtime against Oakland in the Foxboro Stadium finale, the 23-yarder that beat the Raiders in that divisional playoff matchup, and the 48-yarder as time expired to win Super Bowl XXXVI over St. Louis.

But he's still rolling.

"We've got the best weapon in football," Woody said of Vinatieri. "Some offenses need to reach the 20 to be sure of three [points], but we can get to the 40 and have confidence like no one else."

Vinatieri said he tries to make it look like nothing bothers him.

"It's nice to be on a roll again, and what's important is to know your limits and having good communication with the coach," he said.

"I can tell him my range under various conditions after figuring them out the best I can. It's nice to practice in this stadium, where you get a lot of experience with the wind."

OPPOSITE: Kicker Adam Vinatieri has been a model of consistency for the Patriots, especially in clutch situations. (Michael Seamans/Boston Herald)

NEW ENGLAND 19

GAME SEVEN

MIAMI 13

PATS FINALLY BEAT HEAT
OT win stifles swoon in Miami

BY MICHAEL FELGER, BOSTON HERALD

At least one curse is over.

In a game that will take its place among the growing number of improbable last-minute victories under Bill Belichick and Tom Brady, the Patriots defeated the Miami Dolphins, 19-13, in overtime to assume first place in the AFC East. It was the Pats' first-ever win over the Dolphins in Miami in September or October.

The result reaffirmed many things: That Brady can throw it deep and Troy Brown can go get it. That Richard Seymour means more to the Pats than anyone may realize. That Dolphins coach Dave Wannstedt and his team still have problems in the clutch. And that the Pats, despite all the injuries and all the inexperience, just may be on to something special.

"It's like the AFC championship game. Like the Super Bowl," said linebacker Mike Vrabel, who then regained some perspective. "For this time of the season, I mean. We've got a long way to go, but it was still something we've never done before."

Added receiver David Patten: "Everyone's back on the bandwagon! Right back on the bandwagon!"

The game winner was a thing of beauty. With just under six minutes left in overtime, Brady faked a handoff, twirled, faked a slant, then stepped back in the pocket and lofted a perfectly thrown 82-yard bomb to a streaking Brown, who split the Dolphins' two-deep safety coverage with a post pattern.

It was an excellent call by the coaches, who rarely send Brown deep. In fact, Brady spent most of the game looking at other receivers, only giving Brown the ball on quick looks at the line of scrimmage.

Dolphins players said they hadn't seen the Pats run the play on film all year. Slow-footed Dolphins safety Sammy Knight was clearly left ill-prepared.

As for Brady's sore throwing shoulder? Uh, never mind.

"It worked," said Brady. "The [offensive line] gave me a little extra time, I laid it out there and let old little 80 trot in for the score."

Belichick was certainly impressed.

"What a play. What a play," said the coach. "What a throw, what a catch, what a big playmaker Troy Brown is."

As for Brown's complaints that he wasn't seeing the ball enough? Again, never mind.

"They were playing cover two. He threw the ball and I was able to make a play on it," said Brown. "And I just kept running. I'm relieved to be off the field."

The play was possible only because Miami's ultra-clutch kicker, Olindo Mare, saw a 35-yard field goal attempt blocked by Seymour with two minutes left in regulation and another 35-yarder in overtime sail wide right.

Mare, who did not meet the press after the game, had only one kick blocked in his career prior to Seymour's swat. Mare may have been affected by hav-

No. 54 Tedy Bruschi takes down the Dolphins'
Ricky Williams, keeping him under 100 yards on the
day. (Matthew West/Boston Herald)

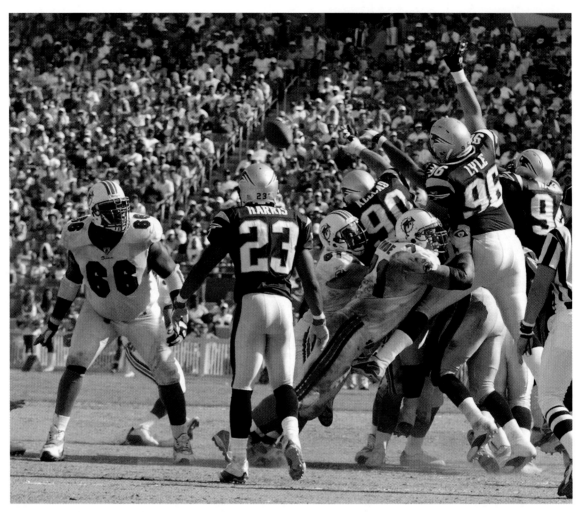

Patriots special teams came up big with a block on an Olindo Mare field goal attempt at the end of regulation, sending the game into overtime. (Matthew West/Boston Herald)

ing to kick off the infield dirt left by the Florida Marlins, but the consensus was that Seymour's first block influenced the overtime miss. Dolphins defensive tackle Larry Chester said Mare was "rattled."

"He was thinking about it," said Seymour, who noticed that Mare tried to lift the second kick after driving at the first.

Added Dolphins special teams coach Keith Armstrong: "I can't tell you right now because I didn't watch the tape and I don't want to nail anybody in the paper."

The Pats' offense had its usual troubles against the Dolphins, fumbling twice and buckling under some curiously conservative play calling from coordinator Charlie Weis down the stretch. But Brady was outstanding, holding up under constant pressure to complete 24-of-34 passes for 283 yards. His 24-yard touchdown pass to David Givens on third down late in the third quarter tied the game.

The defense, meanwhile, was staunch. Ricky Williams (94 yards on 27 carries) didn't really get on track until it was too late, and Jay Fiedler had only one reliable option: tight end Randy McMichael, who was immense, catching eight passes for 102 yards.

In the end, the Pats made the plays when they had to and they came away with the win. Special teams, defense and opportunistic offense carried the day. Sound familiar?

"I can't give enough credit to our guys," said Belichick. "That's a special group of guys."

As such, many players were sure to put the win in perspective. Yes, it ended the Pats' Miami curse and put them in first place. But a look at the calendar showed October, not January.

"We got it done. Cool," said linebacker Tedy Bruschi. "Now let's move on."

Tom Brady fires the game-winning 82-yard TD pass to Troy Brown to beat the Dolphins 19-13 in overtime. (Matthew West/Boston Herald)

	1st	2nd	3rd	4th	OT	Final
New England	3	3	7	0	6	19
Miami	0	10	3	0	0	13

SCORING SUMMARY

Qtr	Team	Play		Time
1	Patriots	FG	Vinatieri 25-yd.	2:24
2	Dolphins	TD	Chambers 6-yd. pass from Fiedler (Mare kick)	10:03
2	Dolphins	FG	Mare 23-yd.	5:08
2	Patriots	FG	Vinatieri 30-yd.	0:02
3	Dolphins	FG	Mare 34-yd.	9:46
3	Patriots	TD	Givens 24-yd. pass from Brady (Vinatieri kick)	1:49
OT	Patriots	TD	T. Brown 82-yd. pass from Brady	5:45

OFFENSE

PATRIOTS

PASSING	COMP	ATT	YDS	TD	INT
Brady	24	34	283	2	0

RECEIVING	REC	YDS	TD
T. Brown	6	131	1
Branch	6	62	0
Givens	3	34	1
Faulk	5	31	0
Fauria	2	16	0
Graham	2	9	0

RUSHING	ATT	YDS	TD
Faulk	18	38	0
Brady	3	10	0
Cloud	5	8	0
McCrary	2	3	0
Klecko	1	0	0

DOLPHINS

PASSING	COMP	ATT	YDS	TD	INT
Fiedler	20	35	230	1	2

RECEIVING	REC	YDS	TD
McMichael	8	102	0
Thompson	3	65	0
Chambers	3	30	1
McKnight	1	16	0
Williams	2	9	0
Ayanbadejo	3	8	0

RUSHING	ATT	YDS	TD
Williams	27	94	0
Fiedler	1	5	0
Ayanbadejo	1	-2	0

Troy Brown rejoices as he scores
the game-winning TD in overtime.
(Matthew West/Boston Herald)

CLEVELAND 3

GAME EIGHT

NEW ENGLAND 9

BROWNOUT
Defense electric in 9-3 victory

BY MICHAEL FELGER, BOSTON HERALD

Call it ugly. Call it uninteresting and unpleasant to watch. Just don't call it unworthy.

On a day when the bubble burst on more than one first-place team in the NFL (Dallas, Minnesota and Seattle all lost), the Pats remained ensconced atop the AFC East with a 9-3 win over Cleveland at blustery and wet Gillette Stadium.

If the win in Miami was worth writing home about, then this result deserved a postcard. But they added up to one thing: a 6-2 record at the season's midpoint. Given the way the year started (Lawyer Milloy's release and a blowout loss in Buffalo) and the injuries that have piled up since (11 starters have missed time), no Patriots' fan should turn a nose up at that.

"We'll take it. 6-2 and headed to Denver on Monday night," center Damien Woody said. "What more could you ask for?"

Some fans could ask for a little offense, but the truth is that the Pats don't need it right now. The defense is playing that well.

"Everybody buys into the team aspect," defensive coordinator Romeo Crennel said. "Like I tell them in the meetings, when everyone's on the same page, then they're pretty good. When they're not on the same page, then we're not very good."

In fairness, the weather was a big factor. And the Browns, who were without starting running back William Green and four projected starters on the offensive line, are a shadow of their 2002-playoff selves.

But three points is three points. Fittingly, cornerback Ty Law, who had his sprained right ankle in a cast early last week, made the game-clinching interception on the Pats' 25-yard line with a minute left.

"You just can't say enough about that group," Pats coach Bill Belichick said. "Any time you hold a team to three points, that's more than one guy doing it. In the end it was enough, that's all you're looking for in this league. Just find a way to win."

The defensive star of the day was linebacker Mike Vrabel, and his plight is symbolic of the unit. Vrabel is playing through a broken bone in his right wrist. He sat out a few games earlier this month, but now he's back even though the break hasn't fully healed. He says he feels it on every play.

Vrabel is an Akron, Ohio, native and former Browns fan ("I was a Dawg-Pounder," he said). But, he bit into the team of his childhood for three sacks, a pass defended and a forced fumble.

"This is why I came back [early]," Vrabel said. "To be a part of this team and be a part of what we're doing."

The Pats knew before the game that Tim Couch would be starting over Kelly Holcomb, but they were hardly surprised when Holcomb came in for the injured Couch (sprained thumb) in the second quarter. In the

Dan Klecko (left) and Richard Seymour team up
to sack Kelly Holcomb on the Browns' final
drive. (Michael Seamans/Boston Herald)

The Patriots' defense celebrates after No. 24 Ty Law comes up with the game-clinching interception. (Matthew West/Boston Herald)

end, it didn't matter, as a Browns offense that Belichick called "very explosive" managed to get past the 50-yard line just once all day.

Unfortunately for the Pats, their offense was only marginally better. The Pats chalked up 19 first downs, but their three trips inside the red zone netted them only a pair of field goals. Things started well enough—Tom Brady hit Bethel Johnson with a beautiful 45-yard bomb on the Pats' first play—but it was downhill from there.

The offense was reduced to three field goals by Adam Vinatieri (27, 28 and 38 yards). A fourth was wiped out on a motion penalty on Dan Koppen.

"Some of these weeks we're going to have to score more points," Brady said. "At some point, that's going to bite us in the butts. I could care less about the defense. I'm more concerned how the offense is playing."

Brady was only half-joking when he said it. Some of his teammates, though, were grateful.

"It's not always going to be pretty," left tackle Matt Light said. "Those guys are paid, too. That's why it's a team sport. That's why when we suit up we wear the same uniform."

Running back Kevin Faulk, who got the start over Antowain Smith, had a career day with 96 yards on 23 carries (4.2-yard average). Ditto second-year tight end Daniel Graham, who had 110 yards on seven catches.

It all added up to the Pats' sixth win in the seven games since Buffalo. Very few people gave the Pats a chance to have that kind of run, and even fewer remained on the bandwagon once the injuries started piling up. But the Pats assumed a "no respect" theme early on, and every week they're sounding more and more like the us-against-the-world 2001 Super Bowl champions.

"We'll be under the radar; that's fine with us," defensive tackle Richard Seymour said. "The only thing that matters is the end of the season—where you're at."

Running back Kevin Faulk breaks into
the open on a second-quarter carry.
Faulk averaged 4.2 yards in the game.
(Michael Seamans/Boston Herald)

	1st	2nd	3rd	4th	Final
Cleveland	0	3	0	0	3
New England	3	0	3	3	9

SCORING SUMMARY

Qtr	Team	Play		Time
1	Patriots	FG	Vinatieri 27-yd.	11:46
2	Browns	FG	Dawson 29-yd.	0:24
3	Patriots	FG	Vinatieri 28-yd.	3:36
4	Patriots	FG	Vinatieri 38-yd.	2:05

OFFENSE

BROWNS

PASSING	COMP	ATT	YDS	TD	INT
Holcomb	15	25	115	0	1
Couch	7	11	40	0	0

RECEIVING	REC		YDS		TD
Davis	3		36		0
Heiden	6		34		0
Johnson	5		30		0
Northcutt	2		29		0
White	3		20		0
Jackson	2		4		0
Morgan	1		2		0

RUSHING	ATT		YDS		TD
Jackson	15		71		0
Boyer	1		7		0
White	2		4		0
Morgan	1		2		0

PATRIOTS

PASSING	COMP	ATT	YDS	TD	INT
Brady	20	33	259	0	0

RECEIVING	REC		YDS		TD
Graham	7		110		0
Faulk	6		58		0
B. Johnson	2		51		0
Branch	3		30		0
T. Brown	2		10		0

RUSHING	ATT		YDS		TD
Faulk	23		96		0
Smith	3		9		0
T. Brown	1		3		0
Brady	2		-2		0
B. Johnson	1		-12		0

Rookie wide receiver Bethel Johnson
runs for extra yardage in the third.
(Matthew West/Boston Herald)

WILLIE McGINEST

MR. VERSATILE

BY RICH THOMPSON, BOSTON HERALD

Willie McGinest has learned to adapt his game to fit the system and, when not hobbled by injuries, is capable of being a disruptive force. His ability to play two positions—outside linebacker and defensive end—has been the hallmark of McGinest's staying power in New England.

"I've been doing it for 10 years, man, so it's not a big deal," said McGinest after morning practice at Gillette Stadium. "We have a lot of versatile guys, and the type of schemes we play is formatted for guys to play different positions, not just me. I can go in at end in some defenses, and the coaches look for that in guys. You've got to do what you've got to do. If the defense calls for it that week, I've got to do it."

Belichick became aware of McGinest's adaptability while serving as Bill Parcells' defensive backs coach during the Patriots' Super Bowl run in 1996. McGinest, who was the Patriots' first-round pick out of USC in 1994, built his reputation as a pass rushing defensive end.

Parcells was partial to hard-charging weak-side linebackers. He had won a pair of Super Bowls using Lawrence Taylor in that capacity with the New York Giants. McGinest was converted to linebacker in his rookie season and thrived in that capacity. In 1995, McGinest started 16 games and recorded 88 tackles and a career-high 11 sacks.

McGinest returned to defensive end for the Patriots' Super Bowl run in 1996 and posted similar numbers from the down position. He finished the season with 67 tackles and 9 1/2 sacks and was elected to represent in the Pats in the Pro Bowl.

"When I came into the NFL at the draft I was a 'tweener between end and linebacker, so playing both is not really a problem for me," McGinest said. "I played the five-technique in Parcells' scheme even though I was a little small for it. Wherever the coach puts me at, I've got to do it."

McGinest has extended his career by fitting into any coach's agenda. McGinest spent three seasons as the Patriots' "elephant" in Pete Carroll's adaptation of the zone blitz.

That system allowed McGinest to freelance on either side of the line to either rush the passer or drop into coverage.

Belichick employs a system that plays to McGinest's strengths without overtaxing his abilities.

"Willie is a pro and he knows the game. He knows how to play his role. I think he has, probably with his experience, gained an appreciation of doing his job and not trying to make every play and not try to play way out of the scheme. He is trying to play within the context of his responsibilities. I think that is a maturity level he has gained."

Veteran Pro Bowler Willie McGinest has adapted to three different coaching systems over his decade-long career. (Michael Seamans/Boston Herald)

NOVEMBER 3, 2003 • INVESCO FIELD

NEW ENGLAND 30

GAME NINE

DENVER 26

PATS GO ABOVE AND BEYOND
Improbable win is best of the bunch

BY KEVIN MANNIX, BOSTON HERALD

These Patriots outdid themselves. The 30-26 victory over the Broncos went beyond the grit, determination, resiliency and all of the other intangibles that have marked the Patriots' success this year. Well beyond.

They showed last night that they CAN win with offense, even against a Denver team that was second in the league in total defense and fifth against the pass. The resilience and heart and coaching (how about that deliberate safety at the end of the game) have been there all along. Last night the offense kicked in, particularly in the passing game.

Even though David Patten didn't play because of a knee injury and Troy Brown gutted it out and played on a sore leg that had him listed as "doubtful" for the game, the pass offense was so good it offset another sloppy overall effort (14 more penalties).

Tom Brady made it happen with a major league performance that should quell all the doubts. He made his usual complement of short passes, screens and slants. But he also made the long passes, completing a 66-yarder for a touchdown, and had two other perfect deep throws go incomplete and intercepted because the receivers couldn't come up with the plays.

For the game he completed 20-of-35 pass attempts for 350 yards, three touchdowns and one tipped interception early in the game.

Late in the game, however, there were no interceptions and no tipped balls. Just big plays under pressure down the stretch as Brady completed 4-of-5 attempts for 58 yards. The final completion was an 18-yard throw to David Givens, who made a diving catch at the left front corner of the end zone.

"This shows that this team has a lot of heart," Givens said. "And we definitely showed that we can win under a lot of circumstances. We found a way to win."

We've known all along that this is a terrific collection of gritty performers. Last night's win went beyond that. And not strictly because of Brady's brilliance down the stretch. But that was certainly the overriding factor.

The Broncos put a decent amount of pressure on him for most of the fourth quarter, but he found a way to slide into an open area and deliver the ball to the right player at the right time. After firing three straight incompletions from his 1-yard line on the next-to-last possession, Brady got another chance after the defense forced a quick Denver punt. If the Broncos had picked up a first down on that series, the Patriots' winning streak would have been over.

OPPOSITE: Adam Vinatieri celebrates his third of three field goals en route to a four-point win over Denver. (Michael Seamans/Boston Herald)

David Givens hauls in the game-winning touchdown in the final seconds of the fourth quarter.
(Michael Seamans/Boston Herald)

Instead, the defense came up big and the Pats have a five-game winning streak going into their bye week.

Another team, at another time, couldn't have won this game.

The Pats had 14 penalties, nine of them coming in the first half. They converted only 3-of-12 third-down situations. They turned the ball over in their own end twice on their first five plays. But somehow, they trailed only 17-13 at the half even though they didn't have a third down conversion and ran only 19 plays to Denver's 40.

Brady completed only five of his 11 pass attempts in the first half, but they were good for 141 yards and that 66-yard touchdown strike to Deion Branch. They fell behind, 17-10, when Denver went 72 yards in 14 plays and scored with 24 seconds left before the break.

But rookie Bethel Johnson returned the kickoff 63 yards to the Broncos' 36 and Adam Vinatieri converted a 46-yard field goal to make it 17-13.

It was just one big play on a night of many.

> **"This shows that this team has a lot of heart. And we definitely showed that we can win under a lot of circumstances. We found a way to win."**
>
> —Patriots wide receiver David Givens

Tom Brady goes deep in the fourth. Brady completed 20-of-35 passes for 350 yards. (Michael Seamans/Boston Herald)

	1st	2nd	3rd	4th	Final
New England	7	6	7	10	30
Denver	7	10	7	2	26

SCORING SUMMARY

Qtr	Team	Play		Time
1	Broncos	TD	Portis 15-yd. run (Elam kick)	10:51
1	Patriots	TD	Branch 66-yd. pass from Brady (Vinatieri kick)	5:55
2	Broncos	FG	Elam 43-yd.	11:29
2	Patriots	FG	Vinatieri 40-yd.	7:57
2	Broncos	TD	Anderson 1-yd. pass from Kanell (Knorr kick)	0:24
2	Patriots	FG	Vinatieri 46-yd.	0:01
3	Patriots	TD	Graham 6-yd. pass from Brady (Vinatieri kick)	5:57
3	Broncos	TD	O'Neal 57-yd. punt return (Knorr kick)	3:13
4	Patriots	FG	Vinatieri 28-yd.	11:08
4	Broncos		Safety	2:49
4	Patriots	TD	Givens 18-yd. pass from Brady (Vinatieri kick)	0:30

OFFENSE

PATRIOTS

PASSING	COMP	ATT	YDS	TD	INT
Brady	20	35	350	3	1

RECEIVING	REC	YDS	TD
Branch	3	107	1
Givens	3	87	1
Faulk	5	52	0
Graham	4	39	1
Fauria	2	30	0
Smith	2	26	0
McCrary	1	9	0

RUSHING	ATT	YDS	TD
Smith	17	55	0
Faulk	5	20	0
Paxton	1	0	0
Walter	1	0	0
Brady	2	-1	0
T. Brown	1	-5	0

BRONCOS

PASSING	COMP	ATT	YDS	TD	INT
Kanell	16	35	163	1	1

RECEIVING	REC	YDS	TD
Smith	4	58	0
Sharpe	3	44	0
Lelie	3	22	0
Portis	4	20	0
Cole	1	18	0
Anderson	1	1	1

RUSHING	ATT	YDS	TD
Portis	26	111	1
Griffin	3	3	0

No. 54 Tedy Bruschi pulls down Clinton Portis in the second half. (Michael Seamans/Boston Herald)

DALLAS 0

GAME TEN

NEW ENGLAND 12

PATS SLAM TUNA, 'BOYS
Defense strong in 12-0 shutout

BY MICHAEL FELGER, BOSTON HERALD

Bill Parcells walked onto the field for pregame warmups at Gillette Stadium to the strains of Pearl Jam's "Dissident."

The Dallas Cowboys' head coach, and onetime Patriots dissenter, then spent several minutes standing alone near midfield, exchanging quick greetings with acquaintances from his former team. Bill Belichick was not among them. ESPN cameras showed Parcells looking to the Pats' side, presumably at Belichick, although neither made a move.

That was the pregame standoff.

The postgame detente came when the two coaches pushed through a throng of cameras at midfield and exchanged a robust hug.

In between, the Pats survived a war of attrition and posted a 12-0 victory, their first shutout of the Belichick era and the franchise's first since 1996. It wasn't pretty, but it surely did the trick for Belichick, who saw his team win its sixth straight game while denying his nemesis another Tuna Bowl victory.

"Bill congratulated me on the win, and I told him he had a good football team," said Belichick, who hadn't spoken to Parcells since the two had a quick conversation at the owners' meetings in March. "I wished him well, and I do."

"I'm about tired of talking about that kind of thing," Parcells said. "The guy did a hell of a job for me for a long time. People in the media can try and

drive a stake between us if they want to, but that's not going to happen on my point—for sure. OK?"

There wasn't much in the way of details, as the Pats capitalized on two long passes from Tom Brady in the first half (thanks to solid maximum-protection schemes) and made a trio of key defensive plays to preserve the shutout in the second half. Those expecting fireworks were disappointed. Those looking for another solid, hard-working effort from the defense were satisfied.

Can the Pats defense play any better?

"That's a good question," defensive coordinator Romeo Crennel said. "We got a shutout, so you've got to be happy with that, but as a coach you can always find something."

Thanks to Crennel's unit, the Pats (8-2) remain squarely atop the mix in the AFC playoff race. They are tied with Indianapolis and Tennessee for the second-best record in the conference. Those three teams now are just one game behind Kansas City (9-1).

Some Pats players admitted the win probably meant a little more to Belichick and his staff than other regular-season victories.

"I'd like to say, normally, no, it wouldn't mean anything more to [Belichick]," linebacker Mike Vrabel said. "But deep down inside—it's like Bobby Fischer beating [Boris Spassky]. I'd say 99.9 percent of the time, as crazy as Belichick is, it wouldn't be any different. It

Tedy Bruschi and the rest of the defense celebrate a
key fourth-and-inches stop of No. 42 Troy Hambrick
late in the game. (Michael Seamans/Boston Herald)

Patriots quarterback Tom Brady aims a bullet pass downfield. Brady went 15-for-34 but was able to connect with receivers for 46-yard and 54-yard bombs that set up scoring opportunities. (Matthew West/Boston Herald)

would just be another win, but I think maybe it did mean a little more."

"Sure, I think it's a big win for all of our coaching staff," linebacker Tedy Bruschi added. "Going against someone you used to work for—if I worked for a guy as long as they worked for that guy, I'd want to beat him, too. It's common sense. I'm sure it feels good to them."

As for the action, there wasn't much. Twice in the first half, the Pats were able to pick up the blitz and go deep, leading to a 46-yard pass play to Deion Branch (setting up an Adam Vinatieri field goal) and a 57-yard completion to David Givens. The pass to Givens, who had to come back for the ball, set up a 2-yard Antowain Smith drive into the end zone—the game's only touchdown.

In the second half, the Cowboys mustered one true scoring threat when they found themselves with a first down on the Pats' 22-yard line. That's when Willie McGinest got in Quincy Carter's face on a rollout, and

Carter's pass to Jason Witten was deflected right into the arms of Ty Law for the first of his two interceptions.

The defense came up with another big stop in the fourth quarter when, on fourth-and-inches, Cowboys running back Troy Hambrick was stopped for a 2-yard loss on a diving tackle by Bruschi. On the Cowboys' next series, Tyrone Poole stepped in front of a seam pass to Terry Glenn (one catch, eight yards) and came down with the interception. Law's interception in the end zone as time expired sealed the win.

Carter finished the night with a measly 38.0 quarterback rating, while the Cowboys were held to 84 yards as a team. Once again, the Pats' defense was the story, and they didn't even need the Bill Bowl to motivate them.

"Belichick's got us playing hard for him, regardless," Vrabel said. "We've got a lot of trust in everything the staff is doing and the positions they're putting us in. We play hard for him anyway. We're at that position where we trust everything they're doing."

"Belichick's got us playing hard for him, regardless."

—Patriots linebacker Mike Vrabel

Surrounded by the media, Cowboys coach Bill Parcells and Patriots coach Bill Belichick put aside their differences and embrace after the game. (Matthew West/Boston Herald)

	1st	2nd	3rd	4th	Final
Dallas	0	0	0	0	0
New England	3	6	0	3	12

SCORING SUMMARY

Qtr	Team	Play		Time
1	Patriots	FG	Vinatieri 23-yd.	3:05
2	Patriots	TD	Smith 2-yd. run	2:34
4	Patriots	FG	Vinatieri 26-yd.	1:56

OFFENSE

COWBOYS

PASSING	COMP	ATT	YDS	TD	INT
Carter	20	36	210	0	3

RECEIVING	REC	YDS	TD
Anderson	8	85	0
Smith	2	38	0
Bryant	3	35	0
Hambrick	2	16	0
Campbell	1	12	0
Murrell	2	10	0
Glenn	1	8	0
Witten	1	6	0

RUSHING	ATT	YDS	TD
Hambrick	16	41	0
Carter	6	33	0
Murrell	3	11	0
Bryant	1	2	0
Anderson	2	-3	0

PATRIOTS

PASSING	COMP	ATT	YDS	TD	INT
Brady	15	34	212	0	0

RECEIVING	REC	YDS	TD
Branch	2	69	0
Givens	2	67	0
Fauria	3	24	0
Faulk	3	22	0
B. Johnson	1	16	0
Pass	2	7	0
Graham	1	5	0
Smith	1	2	0

RUSHING	ATT	YDS	TD
Smith	16	51	1
Faulk	8	11	0
Brady	1	3	0

Deion Branch heads downfield in the first half
on a catch that set up the Pats' first score of
the game. (Michael Seamans/Boston Herald)

BILL BELICHICK

BLAND IS BEAUTIFUL

BY GERRY CALLAHAN, BOSTON HERALD

At this rate, they will be making a movie about his life soon enough, an unlikely story of a charismatically challenged outcast who inspires and motivates a football team in his own odd and inimitable way.

They could call it *Bad Radio*. Or *Bad TV* or *Bad Press Conference* or *Bad Copy* or maybe just *Bad Sport*, the story of a professional football coach who refuses to gloat or pound his chest or dance on the graves of his many victims. They could start with the Cowboys game, when Bill Belichick prevailed in an NFL grudge match of epic proportions, an over-hyped showdown against his former Master and Commander, Bill Parcells.

It was a methodical, professional, businesslike, 12-0 victory for Belichick's Patriots, their sixth straight win and eighth of the season.

And maybe the genius of Belichick is as simple as this: All football coaches say it. This one means it. His players know he will check his emotions and his ego at the door—even on a Sunday night against the great Parcells—and focus on the Xs and Os.

All coaches strive to avoid the extreme highs and lows in the regular season and to keep their teams on an even keel emotionally. Belichick teaches by example. He inspires through preparation, repetition and hard work. If you want wall-shaking oratory, rent *Remember the Titans*. Or hire Mike Ditka. He needs the work. You won't

see Belichick in a TV commercial for a Cadillac dealer or a steakhouse. He is a little busy preparing his team.

Which brings us to the most significant benefit of Belichick's unique style and the one thing that separates him from Parcells. This system is built for the long haul. Unlike some coaches, Belichick doesn't have to come up each week with another dying fan whose last wish is a victory from his beloved football team. All it takes is another good, solid, smart game plan, and Belichick and his staff have always been able to come up with those.

The Belichick formula allows the Patriots to withstand brushfires that might burn lesser teams to the ground. When ESPN's Tom Jackson said, after the season-opening loss in Buffalo, that the New England players "hate their coach," Belichick reacted the only way he knows how. He brushed it off. He hunkered down with his coaches and came up with a game plan. He gave it to his players, and they went out and crushed Philadelphia in Week 2.

We know now that Jackson, who admitted he talked to no one in New England before assessing the player-coach dynamic here, was just speaking out of his rear end, but the point is, it didn't matter.

Life goes on exactly the way the frumpy guy in the gray sweatshirt planned it.

OPPOSITE: Bill Belichick may be frumpy, but his game plans get the job done. (Michael Seamans/Boston Herald)

NEW ENGLAND 23

GAME ELEVEN

HOUSTON 20

AGAIN, PATS PULL THROUGH
Consistent defensive play picks up slack

BY KEVIN MANNIX, BOSTON HERALD

The Patriots keep losing everything but games.

They lost two more coin flips at Reliant Stadium—one to start the game, one at the beginning of overtime. They've now lost 11 straight coin flips, including two at the start of overtime.

They lost four more turnovers, saw Adam Vinatieri miss the first field goal attempt of his career inside a dome after making 30 straight. They saw Vinatieri have a potential game winner in overtime blocked.

For all that, for all of the offensive mistakes and gnarly situations they endured, the Patriots managed to win another game—their seventh straight—with a 23-20 victory over the Texans.

We keep waiting for the string to end, for that other shoe to drop, for the magic powder that's been swirling around these guys to turn to sawdust.

But that's disrespecting these players, coaches and their attitudes.

This isn't magic or karma or destiny. This is about a group of players who live by the old UMass basketball slogan, "Refuse to Lose."

Some teams can't overcome adversity of any degree. Some hope somebody wearing the same color uniform will come through when they need to. These Patriots KNOW something good will happen. It's just a matter of time.

Vinatieri will make a kick. Tom Brady will make a throw. And while they can usually rely on Troy Brown to make a catch, with him out with a bad leg for the last three weeks, people such as Daniel Graham and Deion Branch step up.

And everybody KNOWS the defense will keep hammering away. Somebody—Willie McGinest or Ty Law or Richard Seymour or Rodney Harrison or Mike Vrabel—somebody—will make a big play.

That's been the one constant of this winning streak. The defense has found a way to overcome shortcomings in other areas. The Texans are a reasonable facsimile of an NFL offense, ranked in the middle of the pack in most categories. Against the Patriots they were never competitive, gaining 159 yards on 58 plays.

"That's the thing about this team," said linebacker Ted Johnson, who had his most extensive playing time of the season. "We never lose our cool. We never panic. There's just the feeling in here that we're going to do it. It's not always pretty and it's sure not easy, but we feel confident that somehow we're going to make things happen.

OPPOSITE: Kicker Adam Vinatieri (left) and quarterback Tom Brady celebrate Vinatieri's 28-yard, game-winning field goal in overtime. (Michael Seamans/Boston Herald)

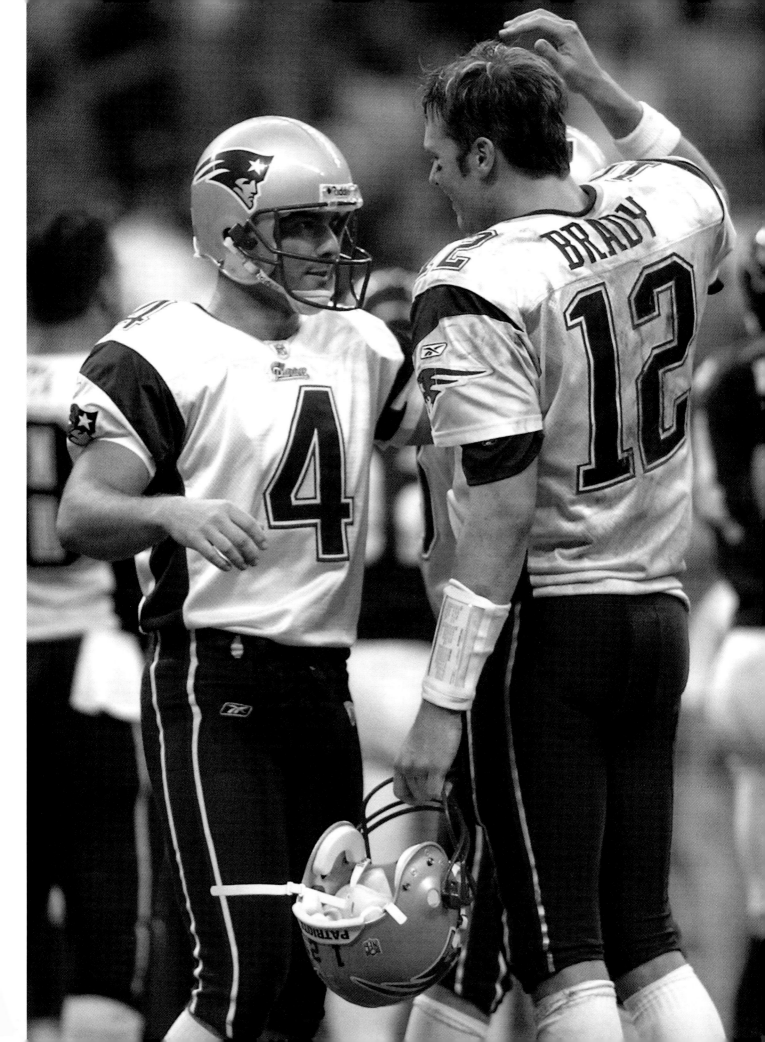

Patriot receiver Bethel Johnson drags No. 24 Eric Brown into the end zone for a second-quarter touchdown. (Michael Seamans/Boston Herald)

"We know that eventually we'll have to play sound football throughout the game. Teams will play us better and not make mistakes when they get a chance to make points.

"Still, the feeling in this locker room is that when we find ourselves in tough situations, we know how to handle it and usually we get it done."

Basically, that's the result of championship defense, the kind the Pats played. Led by Seymour (four tackles, one sack, four deflections) and McGinest (eight tackles, one deflection), the Pats' defense had things in control. The whole way. The Texans had the ball 15 times in the game. They gained more than 33 yards on only one possession—a 79-yard drive that ended with a field goal.

When Houston got the ball in overtime, Vrabel picked off Tony Banks' first pass. When the Texans got the ball at the Pats' 35 late in overtime following yet another abysmal Ken Walter punt, this one covering 31 yards, McGinest stepped up. First he stopped Rookie of the Year candidate Domanick Davis for no gain. Then he broke through and nailed him for a 5-yard loss, essentially knocking Houston out of field goal range. When they went deep on third down, Tyrone Poole stayed close enough to Andre Johnson to force an incompletion.

Another quarterback may have completed that pass. Another quarterback might have come through on one or two other occasions when Johnson got open deep. But another quarterback wasn't playing. Banks was. He wasn't up to the challenge.

"Good teams find a way to win games, man," offensive tackle Matt Light said. "And I think we have a really good team."

Hard to argue, man!

"Still, the feeling in this locker room is that when we find ourselves in tough situations, we know how to handle it and usually we get it done."

—Patriots linebacker
Ted Johnson

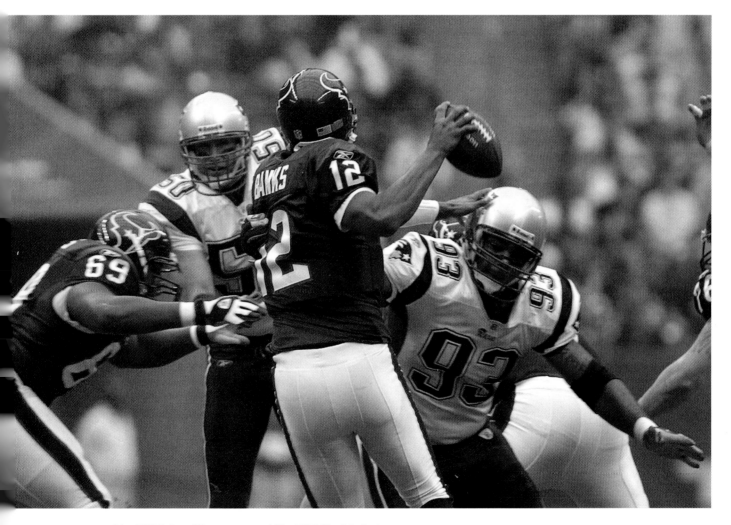

No. 93 Richard Seymour and No. 50 Mike Vrabel
close in on Tony Banks for a sack in the first half.
(Michael Seamans/Boston Herald)

	1st	2nd	3rd	4th	OT	Final
New England	0	10	0	10	3	23
Houston	3	0	7	10	0	20

SCORING SUMMARY

Qtr	Team	Play		Time
1	Texans	FG	Brown 19-yd.	2:36
2	Patriots	TD	B. Johnson 27-yd. pass from Brady (Vinatieri kick)	13:12
2	Patriots	FG	Vinatieri 21-yd.	5:55
3	Texans	TD	Johnson 10-yd. pass from Banks (Brown kick)	4:01
4	Patriots	FG	Vinatieri 32-yd.	14:57
4	Texans	TD	Miller 16-yd. pass from Banks (Brown kick)	6:49
4	Texans	FG	Brown 31-yd.	3:11
4	Patriots	TD	Graham 4-yd. pass from Brady (Vinatieri kick)	0:40
OT	Patriots	FG	Vinatieri 28-yd.	0:41

OFFENSE

PATRIOTS

PASSING	COMP	ATT	YDS	TD	INT
Brady	29	47	368	2	2

RECEIVING	REC	YDS	TD
Faulk	8	108	0
B. Johnson	5	65	1
Graham	4	53	1
Branch	5	52	0
Ward	3	33	0
Stokes	1	31	0
Fauria	1	10	0
Cloud	1	8	0
Pass	1	8	0

RUSHING	ATT	YDS	TD
Faulk	23	80	0
Brady	6	15	0
Pass	2	15	0
Smith	8	10	0
Cloud	2	8	0

TEXANS

PASSING	COMP	ATT	YDS	TD	INT
Banks	10	25	93	2	1

RECEIVING	REC	YDS	TD
Johnson	4	37	1
Bradford	2	19	0
Miller	1	16	1
Armstrong	1	10	0
Davis	1	6	0
Holloway	1	5	0

RUSHING	ATT	YDS	TD
Davis	24	69	0
Gaffney	1	13	0
Banks	2	5	0
Johnson	2	3	0
Hollings	1	-1	0

Mike Vrabel runs back an interception of
Tony Banks' first pass in overtime.
(Michael Seamans/Boston Herald)

NEW ENGLAND 38

GAME TWELVE

INDIANAPOLIS 34

STUFF OF CHAMPIONS
Pats deny Colts on goal line to secure win

BY MICHAEL FELGER, BOSTON HERALD

Is it possible to be a championship-caliber team without a running back you can trust and a punter you can rely on?

Ask the Patriots. They're the Answer Team.

That's the nickname the coaches have given the kickoff return unit, but it really applies to the whole team. And once again, the Pats had an answer.

"This is what championship teams are about," said linebacker Willie McGinest after his fourth-down tackle of Edgerrin James on the 1-yard line capped a heroic goal-line stand and preserved yet another dramatic win for the Pats. "To be the best, you've got to beat the best, and that's what we did."

It was another white-knuckle afternoon of football for the cardiac Patriots, who blew a 21-point second-half lead before hanging on for a 38-34 victory over the Colts at the RCA Dome. Despite a late Kevin Faulk fumble and an 18-yard shank from embattled punter Ken Walter, the Pats won for the eighth consecutive week.

"That was some football game," said coach Bill Belichick. "For our guys to hang in there on the road like that, my hat's off to the players."

There are hundreds of details to dissect, but fans will spend most of their time on the final four minutes. It started with the Pats holding a seven-point lead and with the ball deep in their own territory. That's when Faulk fumbled after a hit from linebacker Marcus Washington, and the Colts took over at the Pats' 11. Three plays later, the Colts had a field goal and the lead was four.

With another chance to run out the clock, but not trusting Faulk to do it, the Pats coaches then called three consecutive pass plays. All were incomplete. Walter then had an opportunity to bail everyone out with a big kick, but instead he produced another duck. The Colts took over at the Pats' 48-yard line and quickly drove down to the 2.

Then it really got interesting. Two runs by James netted 1 yard. On third down, with 18 seconds on the clock, Peyton Manning overthrew Aaron Moorehead in the corner of the end zone, with good coverage from Tyrone Poole. The Colts then called James' number again, this time over the right side, and he was hit initially by nose tackle Ted Washington and then brought down by McGinest. Ball game.

"I've never seen anything like it," said safety Rodney Harrison.

The last play came down to what's been winning games for the Pats all season: coaching and teamwork. Belichick said the Colts had shown the tendency to run James in that situation all year. McGinest said Manning helped tip off the defense when he patted his right hip prior to the snap. And another veteran said that right guard Steve Sciullo tipped off some of the Patriots by the way he put the weight on his right hand as he went into his stance.

No. 83 Deion Branch and David Givens celebrate what
turned out to be the game-winning touchdown.
(Michael Seamans/Boston Herald)

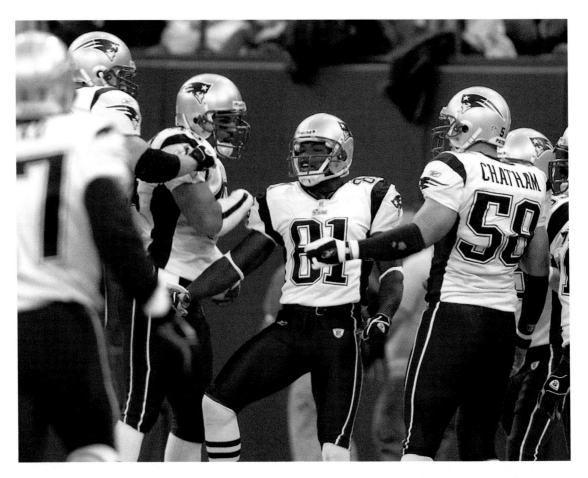

Bethel Johnson (center) is swarmed in the end zone after returning a kickoff for a touchdown to end the first half. (Michael Seamans/Boston Herald)

"Just the way he got down, there was no way that was a pass," said the player.

Meanwhile, the Colts may be looking for answers from McGinest, who fell to the ground in apparent pain just prior to the goal-line stand and forced an official's timeout. McGinest's "injury" forced a clock stoppage (the Pats had no timeouts) and allowed the players valuable time to collect themselves.

Belichick said that McGinest "cramped up at the end there. If the player is hurt, you have to get him off the field."

McGinest said he actually jammed his knee.

"I'm not a faker, dog," he shouted as he left the locker room. "Don't worry about that."

Despite their lofty standing, the Pats certainly have some things to worry about down the stretch. For the first time this season, the Pats' rookies played like rookies, particularly safety Eugene Wilson. Manning was able to throw four touchdowns as a result, bringing the Colts back from deficits of 17-0 and 31-10.

Another developing issue for the Pats is the carelessness of Brady, who was at times brilliant in picking apart the porous Colts defense but also threw two killer second-half interceptions.

Thankfully for Brady and the defense, the Pats had returner Bethel Johnson and the Answer Team to rely on.

The Pats selected the rookie receiver in the second round out of Texas A&M in large part because of the gaudy 40-yard dash times he ran on the same RCA Dome turf at the scouting combine in February (4.2 range). Johnson certainly seemed at home yesterday—his 92-yard touchdown return to end the first half gave the Pats a 24-10 lead, and his 67-yard return in the fourth quarter set up Brady's game-winning 13-yard strike to Deion Branch with 8:36 remaining.

And that's the way it's gone for the Pats this year. Faulk can fumble, Walter can shank and Brady can give the ball away. The Pats will have an answer.

Said Harrison: "We've done it so many times before, why would this one be any different?"

"That was some football game. For our guys to hang in there on the road like that, my hat's off to the players."

—Patriots coach Bill Belichick

Peyton Manning looks to get rid of the ball as Ted Washington closes in on him. (Michael Seamans/Boston Herald)

	1st	2nd	3rd	4th	Final
New England	10	14	7	7	38
Indianapolis	0	10	14	10	34

SCORING SUMMARY

Qtr	Team	Play		Time
1	Patriots	FG	Vinatieri 43-yd.	9:04
1	Patriots	TD	Cloud 4-yd. run (Vinatieri kick)	2:32
2	Patriots	TD	Ward 31-yd. pass from Brady (Vinatieri kick)	11:54
2	Colts	FG	Vanderjagt 40-yd.	7:04
2	Colts	TD	Pollard 8-yd. pass from Manning (Vanderjagt kick)	0:12
2	Patriots	TD	B. Johnson 92-yd. kick return (Vinatieri kick)	0:00
3	Patriots	TD	Cloud 1-yd. run (Vinatieri kick)	7:36
3	Colts	TD	Wayne 13-yd. pass from Manning (Vanderjagt kick)	1:20
3	Colts	TD	Harrison 26-yd. pass from Manning (Vanderjagt kick)	0:14
4	Colts	TD	Walters 6-yd. pass from Manning (Vanderjagt kick)	10:21
4	Patriots	TD	Branch 13-yd. pass from Brady (Vinatieri kick)	8:36
4	Colts	FG	Vanderjagt 29-yd.	3:27

OFFENSE

PATRIOTS

PASSING	COMP	ATT	YDS	TD	INT
Brady	26	35	236	2	2

RECEIVING	REC	YDS	TD
Branch	6	64	1
Ward	2	50	1
Fauria	5	45	0
Faulk	5	36	0
Givens	3	21	0
B. Johnson	2	7	0
Stokes	1	7	0
Pass	1	6	0
Andruzzi	1	0	0

RUSHING	ATT	YDS	TD
Faulk	15	42	0
Pass	2	9	0
Cloud	4	6	2
Brady	2	-1	0

COLTS

PASSING	COMP	ATT	YDS	TD	INT
Manning	29	48	278	4	1

RECEIVING	REC	YDS	TD
Harrison	7	88	1
Walters	5	56	1
James	8	50	0
Pollard	4	36	1
Wayne	3	30	1
Clark	2	18	0

RUSHING	ATT	YDS	TD
James	25	88	0
Rhodes	2	9	0
Manning	2	1	0

No. 55 Willie McGinest and No. 92 Ted Washington
stop Edgerrin James and the Colts on fourth and goal
from the 1-yard line to preserve the win.
(Michael Seamans/Boston Herald)

TOM BRADY

BRADY LETS CLUTCH OUT

BY KAREN GUREGIAN, BOSTON HERALD

There's a line from Kevin Costner's movie *Tin Cup* that talks about athletes and their ability to either rise or fall in the clutch. It went like this: "Either you define the moment, or the moment defines you."

When it comes to the Patriots, we've seen Tom Brady faced with many such moments during his short career.

Tie score. Eighty-one ticks left on the clock. First-and-10 from the 17. No timeouts left. The Super Bowl in the balance.

Three-point deficit. Monday Night Football in Denver. First-and-10 from the 42 with 2:15 to play.

Seven-point deficit. In Houston. First-and-10 from the 15. Third-and-10 from the 33 with 2:26 left. Fourth-and-1 from the 4 with 40 seconds left.

Overtime. Pick just about any situation with the ball during the last seven overtime games played by the Patriots.

These are Brady moments. These are the moments HE defines. These are the moments that have made him the current best NFL quarterback on the planet with the game on the line.

What he's able to do is something that can't be taught or imitated. You can't teach the level of calmness and cool he has amid the pressure and craziness of a game-on-the-line situation. You can't mimic an ability to perform in extreme circumstances. Either you have it or you don't. And Brady definitely has it.

Maybe when you conquer that Super Bowl situation on your first try, when you drive your team from the 17 into field goal position with no timeouts and just over a minute remaining, everything else seems as simple as making a handoff.

Legendary UCLA hoops coach John Wooden once said: "Sports do not build character. They reveal it."

In the case of Brady, it's hard to come up with something better than being known as the quarterback you'd most like to have in a make-or-break situation.

The moments have certainly added up, and he's put his mark on them. Quite simply, he defines clutch.

Quarterback Tom Brady has proven himself time
and time again. (Kuni Takahashi/Boston Herald)

DECEMBER 7, 2003 • GILLETTE STADIUM

MIAMI 0
GAME THIRTEEN
NEW ENGLAND 12

PATRIOTS FREEZE FISH
Clinch AFC East crown with shutout

BY MICHAEL FELGER, BOSTON HERALD

The championship hats and T-shirts were distributed in the postgame locker room, and several Patriots players even wore them for the cameras.

But you could tell no one was impressed.

The Pats certainly have loftier goals than the AFC East title they claimed for the second time in three years. The Pats now own an inside track to the Super Bowl, and the 12-0 shutout over Miami at blustery Gillette Stadium served notice to the rest of the league that their defense isn't just outstanding.

It's dominant.

"We didn't want to prolong the fight," said linebacker Tedy Bruschi moments after his interception return for a touchdown in the fourth quarter sealed the win and induced a wild snowball shower from the 45,378 hearty fans in attendance. "Just finish it today. Get your hats and T-shirts in the locker room and move on."

"They played as hard as they could play," coach Bill Belichick said. "There were so many guys who stepped up and made big play after big play. I'm proud of our players. They played hard and they played well."

It was a heady afternoon for Belichick's crew, and the surreal scene in the stands was only the backdrop.

The Pats (11-2) tied a franchise record for wins in a season while picking up their club-best ninth straight victory. Perhaps most impressively, the Pats have now played seven games against teams with winning records—and they've won all seven of them.

If there's an NFL team playing better than the Pats right now, that team has yet to identify itself.

"Unbelievable," said safety Rodney Harrison, who was a one-man wrecking crew with 11 tackles, a sack and a forced fumble. "What an experience. I'm elated right now."

Everyone on the Pats' defense has a right to feel that way. Not only did the defense keep the Dolphins off the scoreboard, but it outscored the Pats' offense by a resounding 9-3.

"Today we made a statement that we deserve to be considered at the top of the league," linebacker Mike Vrabel said.

The defense was so good, it literally cracked heads. Dolphins guard Jamie Nails found that out when his helmet split in two after a lick from Ted Johnson in the first half.

The Pats got all the points they would need on an Adam Vinatieri 29-yard field goal in the first quarter.

OPPOSITE: In a game-sealing play, Ty Law picks off a pass intended for Dolphin receiver Chris Chambers. (Matthew West/Boston Herald)

96

Jay Fiedler (No. 9 in background) can't bear to watch as Tedy Bruschi and Matt Chatham celebrate Bruschi's interception and touchdown. (Michael Seamans/Boston Herald)

The closest the Dolphins came to denting the scoreboard was in the third quarter, when they advanced to the Pats' 10-yard line. But on third-and-3, Harrison came around left end on a blitz and strip-sacked Jay Fiedler. Richard Seymour recovered and the ball was back in the Pats' court.

Bruschi's 5-yard interception return made it 10-0 with 8:55 remaining, and Jarvis Green's sack of Fiedler in the end zone with 1:13 left sealed the deal.

There were several defensive stars, a list including Ted Washington (10 tackles), Ty Law (three passes defended and an interception), Seymour (five tackles, sack), Vrabel (five tackles, sack, forced fumble, fumble recovery) and Bruschi (six tackles). The collective effort held Miami back Ricky Williams to 68 yards on 25 carries and Fiedler to 13 completions on 31 attempts.

The player who stood head and shoulders above the rest was Harrison. Clearly spurred on by his war of

words with Dolphins tight end Randy McMichael, Harrison was an unstoppable force all game. McMichael finished without a catch.

"Any time someone calls you out and disrespects you, you want to go out and prove to everyone you still have it," Harrison said. "It definitely raises your level."

How much higher can the Pats raise their level? Time will tell. But one thing is for certain: They still don't think they've played their best football.

"I think everything is ahead of us," quarterback Tom Brady said.

"Just one step closer," said Seymour. "We're just starting to jell and look like a football team. It's going to be interesting down the stretch. We know we have a good defense. But we still have to go out and prove it every Sunday. Talking isn't going to get it done."

> "Today we made a statement that
> we deserve to be considered at
> the top of the league."
>
> —Patriots linebacker Mike Vrabel

Tedy Bruschi (left) and Ty Law celebrate Bruschi's
first-half sack. (Michael Seamans/Boston Herald)

	1st	2nd	3rd	4th	Final
Miami	0	0	0	0	0
New England	3	0	0	9	12

SCORING SUMMARY

Qtr	Team	Play		Time
1	Patriots	FG	Vinatieri 29-yd.	1:46
4	Patriots	TD	Bruschi 5-yd. interception return (Vinatieri kick)	8:55
4	Patriots		Safety	1:13

OFFENSE

DOLPHINS

PASSING	COMP	ATT	YDS	TD	INT
Fiedler	13	31	111	0	2

RECEIVING	REC	YDS	TD
Gadsden	2	34	0
Chambers	4	32	0
Thompson	2	31	0
Konrad	2	9	0
Williams	1	5	0
McKnight	1	4	0
Minor	1	-4	0

RUSHING	ATT	YDS	TD
Williams	25	68	0

PATRIOTS

PASSING	COMP	ATT	YDS	TD	INT
Brady	16	31	163	0	0

RECEIVING	REC	YDS	TD
Branch	6	93	0
Graham	6	24	0
Givens	2	17	0
Faulk	1	15	0
Ward	1	14	0

RUSHING	ATT	YDS	TD
Smith	27	60	0
Faulk	5	20	0
Brady	2	-2	0

Pats fans go nuts and throw snow into the air after Tedy Bruschi scored on a fourth-quarter interception. (Michael Seamans/Boston Herald)

JACKSONVILLE 13

GAME FOURTEEN

NEW ENGLAND 27

SNOW WAY TO END STREAK
Patriots defense finally allows TD

BY MICHAEL GEE, BOSTON HERALD

It turned out it took a blizzard to get another team into the Patriots' end zone at Gillette Stadium. Byron Leftwich's wounded duck with 3:22 to play in the game was a classic jump ball. But the snow was coming down so hard neither Patriots defensive back Asante Samuel nor Jaguars wideout Kevin Johnson could see the pigskin.

By literally blind luck, Leftwich's pass settled into Johnson's arms for a Jacksonville touchdown. The Jaguars had gone where no visting man had gone before—not for a long while, anyway.

To be precise, it'd been 301 minutes, 22 seconds of playing time and 337 enemy plays since the Pats had surrendered a touchdown at home, way back on Oct. 5, when Tennessee's Steve McNair scored in the Patriots' 38-30 victory, the first of what's now a 10-game winning streak.

Or to put it another way, the last time the Pats allowed a touchdown at home, Grady Little still had a job.

So, Johnson's fourth-quarter score was a noteworthy accomplishment, albeit an irrelevant one.

"The streak's over," said Pats linebacker Tedi Bruschi. "What was the [expletive] score?"

That would be New England 27, Jacksonville 13. The Patriots' defense had done its job and then some by the time the Jaguars crossed the goal line. A fluky, weather-aided play shouldn't count against the Pats' defenders' record of total dominance in their red zone.

Before the storm hit in the second half yesterday, Bruschi and his mates again got better the less real estate they had to defend.

"Well, you look around and see there's not much room behind you," Bruschi said. "So you've got to do something."

The Jaguars moved the ball more successfully against the Patriots than any visitor since the Titans. Jacksonville's very first play was a 67-yard pass from Leftwich to Jimmy Smith, setting up a first-and-goal from the Patriots' 9-yard line. Three plays later, the Jags kicked a field goal.

On their next possession, the Jaguars drove to first-and-goal on the Patriots' 5. Again, they went three plays and out, forced to settle for three points.

Late in the first half, trailing 13-6, Jags coach Jack Del Rio wouldn't even try to make a fourth-and-2 from the Pats' 16, and Seth Marler missed a 34-yard kick.

The Pats' defense turned 21 potential points allowed into six. They used the Josef Stalin game plan: Hold the enemy out of Moscow until the snows come.

Red-zone defense is creating the Patriots' unusual pattern of victory. The Pats are dominating teams everywhere but the scoreboard, because the board doesn't have a category for "points that should've happened but didn't."

Tom Brady looks downfield and threads the needle.
(Michael Seamans/Boston Herald)

Tyrone Poole (left) and Ty Law celebrate the first of Poole's two interceptions. (Michael Seamans/Boston Herald)

"We're not exactly blowing teams out," quarterback Tom Brady said.

This reporter is willing to bet that the Pats' 10-game win streak is the only one in NFL history in which the largest margin of victory was yesterday's 14 points.

Ordinarily, a team good enough to win 10 straight has one or more routs to its credit. The Pats are winning what must be called anti-routs.

Scores that should happen but don't determine quite as many games as scores that take place. The teams the Pats send home losers all spend much time bemoaning missed opportunities. Actually, those guys have fallen to a defense whose best plays are counterpunches off the ropes.

"It's a matter of pride," said Rodney Harrison, who (surprise!) led the Pats with 11 tackles. "We say they can't win if they don't score. If they get to where they have to score, let's make sure we make it a field goal."

Red-zone defense is pride. Call it passion or effort if that suits you better; it all means the same thing. When football boils down to the simplest matter of pushing and shoving, the Pats' defense is able to impose its will. The team with superior will always wins.

Their scores don't reflect dominance, but that's just what the Pats are. It takes more than a snowstorm to hide them.

"It's a matter of pride. We say they can't win if they don't score. If they get to where they have to score, let's make sure we make it a field goal."

—Patriots safety Rodney Harrison

Running back Antowain Smith leans over the goal line for a fourth-quarter touchdown to make the score 27-6. (Michael Seamans/Boston Herald)

	1st	2nd	3rd	4th	Final
Jacksonville	3	3	0	7	13
New England	7	6	0	14	27

SCORING SUMMARY

Qtr	Team	Play		Time
1	Patriots	TD	Graham 27-yd. pass from Brady (Vinatieri kick)	10:02
1	Jaguars	FG	Marler 24-yd.	7:19
2	Patriots	FG	Vinatieri 22-yd.	14:13
2	Jaguars	FG	Marler 23-yd.	7:18
2	Patriots	FG	Vinatieri 31-yd.	2:30
4	Patriots	TD	T. Brown 10-yd. pass from Brady (Vinatieri kick)	10:57
4	Patriots	TD	Smith 1-yd. run (Vinatieri kick)	4:18
4	Jaguars	TD	Johnson 27-yd. pass from Leftwich (Marler kick)	3:22

OFFENSE

JAGUARS

PASSING	COMP	ATT	YDS	TD	INT
Leftwich	21	40	288	1	2

RECEIVING	REC	YDS	TD
Johnson	5	87	1
Smith	2	73	0
Edwards	4	41	0
Taylor	4	32	0
Luzar	1	21	0
Edwards	1	17	0
Brady	2	8	0
Allen	1	6	0
Hankton	1	3	0

RUSHING	ATT	YDS	TD
Taylor	16	57	0
Leftwich	3	10	0
Allen	1	5	0

PATRIOTS

PASSING	COMP	ATT	YDS	TD	INT
Brady	22	34	228	2	0

RECEIVING	REC	YDS	TD
Graham	5	69	1
Givens	5	65	0
T. Brown	4	43	1
Branch	1	16	0
Faulk	3	9	0
Smith	2	9	0
Ward	1	9	0
Centers	1	8	0

RUSHING	ATT	YDS	TD
Smith	17	39	1
Faulk	11	34	0
Brady	1	7	0
Pass	2	3	0
Centers	1	1	0

Teammates congratulate tight end Daniel Graham on his 27-yard touchdown grab in the first quarter. The Patriots were held to field goals until the beginning of the fourth quarter. (Matthew West/Boston Herald)

CHARLIE WEIS
ROMEO CRENNEL

OFFENSIVE COORDINATOR AND DEFENSIVE COORDINATOR

A COORDINATED EFFORT

BY KAREN GUREGIAN, BOSTON HERALD

Their names are being mentioned as potential candidates with every NFL coach firing or rumored firing. Their mugshots are included prominently in every future candidate lineup.

Given the wealth of vacancies, Patriots players are well aware they could lose one, or both, of their top assistants in the off season.

Pats quarterback Tom Brady is especially fond of Charlie Weis, and though the coach is uneasy speaking about future employment opportunities, the Patriots' QB was quite candid about his feelings.

"I think he's probably the best coach I ever had," Brady said of Weis. "He's extremely hard-working, smart, he always puts us in a great position to do well. He's always prepared, and it does sound like at some point we'll lose him, unfortunately, from everything you hear.

"Especially, with the development and rapport we've had for three or four years. Any time you lose a coach that you respect so much, that would [expletive]. But I think it's a goal of his. At some point it's everyone's goal to reach the top. There's no doubt he's capable. That's obvious."

Romeo Crennel, who is in his 23rd NFL season, seventh as a Patriots' coach, does envision himself as a head coach. Some coordinators are happy being just that and don't want the added responsibility. Not Crennel. He definitely wants the opportunity to run the show.

"Romeo is a very knowledgeable guy. He's really into it. He lives and breathes football. He loves it. A guy like that really deserves an opportunity to be a head coach somewhere," remarked safety Rodney Harrison, who's in the midst of his first season under Crennel. "He pays the price. He's a very knowledgeable guy. He studies hard. He really bleeds it. I believe he's well deserving of consideration."

Many of his players believe he hasn't gotten nearly enough credit for their success over the years.

"He's the glue that keeps the defense together," cornerback Ty Law remarked. "Everyone talks about Coach Belichick every time they mention our defense. But Belichick isn't in our meetings. I think [Crennel] should get more credit for what's going on back there. He's a great coach; he's paid his dues.

"To be honest with you, I'd hate to see him leave, but I think he deserves a shot at being a head coach because he knows how to bring the team together, he knows how to put people in the right situations, he knows what to call in certain situations. He's been second fiddle for a long time. He's got his credit amongst the players, but he's coached a lot longer than other guys who've gotten opportunities. He's coached on Super Bowl champion teams. I just think he should get his just due."

ABOVE: Defensive coordinator Romeo Crennel (left) deserves a lion's share of the credit for this season's success. (Matthew West/Boston Herald)

LEFT: Offensive coordinator Charlie Weis is a player favorite and hopes to become a head coach in the future. (Jessica Rinaldi/Boston Herald)

NEW ENGLAND 21

GAME FIFTEEN

NEW YORK JETS 16

PATS INTERCEPT JETS
Claim 11th straight win

BY MICHAEL FELGER, BOSTON HERALD

Nothing was settled, and everything remains to be determined. All the Patriots did was add another game to their league-best winning streak while upping the pressure on the teams chasing them in the AFC standings.

For now, it will have to do.

Intercepting Jets quarterback Chad Pennington five times while getting a revived effort from running back Antowain Smith, the Pats posted a 21-16 victory over the rival New York Jets at the Meadowlands. The win was the 11th straight for the 13-2 Patriots.

However, there is more work to be done if the Pats are to earn a coveted first-round playoff bye.

"As always, we're happy to win," coach Bill Belichick said. "It wasn't perfect, but it was a good, solid effort. It's a division game on the road. To be able to come down here and get the win—it's definitely a sense of accomplishment."

Motivation won't be a problem against Buffalo next week. The players hadn't even gotten their pads off in the locker room after beating the Jets before Belichick reminded his players of the 31-0 shellacking the Bills put on them in Week 1.

"It's not often you get a chance at redemption," guard Damien Woody said. "Looking at the scoreboard and seeing a big donut, that hasn't left anyone on the team.

"We're definitely looking forward to this upcoming game."

Many players on the Patriots' defense acknowledged they were once again disappointed in their performance last night. The Jets moved the ball well for much of the game, picking up 22 first downs. But while he rushed for two scores, Pennington was his own worst enemy, throwing the ball into the arms of five different Pats defenders.

One interception was returned 15 yards for a touchdown by linebacker Willie McGinest in the second quarter. Another was collected by cornerback Ty Law in the end zone. Another was recorded by linebacker Tedy Bruschi, whose third pick of the season and first not returned for a touchdown came on the game's second play from scrimmage and set up a Pats touchdown. The fifth and final Pennington pick fell into the arms of safety Eugene Wilson with 45 seconds on the clock and the Jets driving for a potential winning score.

OPPOSITE: Rookie cornerback Eugene Wilson and No. 54 Tedy Bruschi celebrate Wilson's pickoff of Chad Pennington to seal the game for the Pats 21-16. (Matthew West/Boston Herald)

**Patriots Richard Seymour and Willie McGinest (top) crunch Jets QB Chad Pennington.
(Matthew West/Boston Herald)**

"I was surprised to see him throw so many interceptions, yeah," Wilson said. "He looked like his head was on a swivel. He seemed pretty boggled out there."

Added nose tackle Ted Washington: "We played well enough, but not great. The turnovers kept us in the game."

The offense also did its part. Particularly Smith, who ran for 121 yards on 18 carries to become the Pats' first 100-yard rusher since November 2002. The Jets came into the game ranked 31st in the league against the run—and the Pats exploited that weakness. Smith was effective from the opening whistle, as he got the start and ran eight times for 58 yards in the first half and 10 times for 63 yards in the second.

Tom Brady was typically efficient, completing 15-of-25 passes for 138 yards and a pair of touchdowns, both to wide receiver David Givens. The first came on the Patriots' first play from scrimmage when Brady side-stepped pressure and found a wide-open Givens along the left sideline for the score. The second Brady-to-Givens touchdown, a 5-yard scoring strike that made the score 21-10, came on the Patriots' first offensive series of the second half.

The Patriots couldn't capitalize on other opportunities to extend the lead, but were at least careful with the ball. The only turnover came on an ill-advised double-reverse pass thrown by Givens. The receiver's underthrown heave was easily picked off by Tyrone Carter.

"We left some points out there as always," Brady said. "But it's still a good win."

Indeed, given the circumstances, the game didn't figure to come down to the end.

"It was the Pats and the Jets," Bruschi said. "You get five turnovers and you score on defense and you think it would be a little easier. But it never is here."

"It was the Pats and the Jets. You get
five turnovers and you score on defense
and you think it would be a little easier.
But it never is here."

—Patriots linebacker Tedy Bruschi

Antowain Smith runs for a big gain in the fourth
quarter. Smith rushed for 121 yards on 18 carries.
(Matthew West/Boston Herald)

	1st	2nd	3rd	4th	Final
New England	7	7	7	0	21
New York Jets	7	3	0	6	16

SCORING SUMMARY

Qtr	Team	Play	....	Time
1	Patriots	TD	Givens 35-yd. pass from Brady (Vinatieri kick)	14:12
1	Jets	TD	Pennington 1-yd. run (Brien kick)	4:52
2	Patriots	TD	McGinest 15-yd. interception return (Vinatieri kick)	13:24
2	Jets	FG	Brien 29-yd.	0:01
3	Patriots	TD	Givens 5-yd. pass from Brady (Vinatieri kick)	10:53
4	Jets	TD	Pennington 10-yd. run (Failed 2-pt conv. attempt)	12:11

OFFENSE

PATRIOTS

PASSING	COMP	ATT	YDS	TD	INT
Brady	15	25	138	2	0
Givens	0	1	0	0	1

RECEIVING	REC	YDS	TD
Givens	4	61	2
T. Brown	4	35	0
Branch	2	24	0
Fauria	1	10	0
Graham	1	4	0
Centers	1	2	0
Smith	2	2	0

RUSHING	ATT	YDS	TD
Smith	18	121	0
Faulk	3	8	0
Centers	1	3	0
Brady	2	1	0

JETS

PASSING	COMP	ATT	YDS	TD	INT
Pennington	24	43	229	0	5

RECEIVING	REC	YDS	TD
Moss	5	52	0
Conway	4	38	0
Lockett	2	34	0
Baker	3	31	0
Becht	4	29	0
Sowell	2	24	0
Martin	4	21	0

RUSHING	ATT	YDS	TD
Martin	22	89	0
Pennington	4	20	2

Linebacker Willie McGinest returns a
Chad Pennington interception 15 yards
for a touchdown in the second quarter.
(Matthew West/Boston Herald)

BUFFALO 0
GAME SIXTEEN
NEW ENGLAND 31

PATS EXACT REVENGE ON BILLS
Secure home field advantage

BY MICHAEL FELGER, BOSTON HERALD

There was no champagne in the locker room, cigars in the hallway or Gatorade shower on the sideline. But that didn't mean the Patriots were oblivious to what they had just accomplished.

"Think about what we just did," owner Bob Kraft, sitting in on Bill Belichick's postgame press conference, said. "We just won 14-of-15 games."

And that meant only one thing.

"The road to the Super Bowl goes through Foxboro," defensive lineman Richard Seymour said. "Everyone knows that."

They know it because the Pats won again, posting a symmetrical and resounding 31-0 shutout on the Buffalo Bills at Gillette Stadium. The win avenged the low-water mark of the Belichick era, a blowout loss in Buffalo on opening day by the same score. The victory also extended a franchise-record winning streak to 12 games.

In NFL history, only two teams have finished the season with a longer winning streak—the perfect 1972 Dolphins and the 1934 Chicago Bears. The Pats finished undefeated at home (8-0) for the first time in franchise history.

Belichick allowed his veterans to enjoy the accomplishment in the waning moments of the game, calling many of his starters off the field one by one to a round of applause from the home crowd. If the players basked in that moment, then it was quickly shelved by the time the locker room doors opened.

"Fourteen and two, 5-1 in the division," a subdued Belichick said. "That's not bad."

The players followed suit.

"Who cares what you did the last 16 games if you go out and lay an egg in the playoffs?" safety Rodney Harrison said. "We're really not patting ourselves on the back right now."

Added linebacker Tedy Bruschi: "The slate is clean."

In the same breath, though, the Pats were honest about what the regular-season finale meant. And that, of course, was revenge for the regular-season opener. Any doubts about that were put to rest in the closing seconds, when Belichick sent out most of his starting goal-line defense with Buffalo set up at the 1. Linebacker Larry Izzo's interception in the end zone preserved the Pats' third home shutout of the season.

"How's that for irony?" Bruschi said of flip-flopping the final score from Week 1 at Buffalo. "Talk about payback. Maybe that's just Foxboro magic."

Added Harrison: "Of course we wanted to go out there and make a statement. We wanted to prove a point."

That point was proven in emphatic fashion. Of course, the woeful Bills were playing out the string and

Maintaining their shutout, the special teams
block a field goal attempt in the second quarter.
(Matthew West/Boston Herald)

QB Drew Bledsoe winces as Rodney Harrison (right) wraps him up in the second quarter for a sack. (Matthew West/Boston Herald)

were in no position to put up a fight. They had the buses idling in the parking lot from the opening kickoff, and the Pats took advantage.

For once, the Patriots' offense set the tone. Opening up with a no-huddle, empty-backfield attack, Tom Brady picked apart the vaunted Buffalo defense, which came into the game as the No. 2-ranked unit and had hopes of vaulting to the top spot. Brady threw four touchdown passes to four receivers (tight end Daniel Graham and wideouts Bethel Johnson, Troy Brown and David Givens) and survived a scary hit to the knee by former teammate Lawyer Milloy in the first half, then put it on autopilot after halftime.

Meanwhile, Drew Bledsoe was atrocious in front of a patchwork Bills offensive line, completing just 12-

of-29 passes for 83 yards, three sacks, an interception and a fumble. He didn't complete a single pass in the first quarter.

"They're a darn good football team right now," said Bledsoe. "And we're not."

Milloy recorded eight tackles and little else from his safety position, and was flagged for pass interference in the end zone to set up the Pats' first score—a 1-yard Brady-to-Graham strike.

"It was a surreal experience," said Milloy. "It was the final steps as far as closure is concerned."

And while Milloy and the Bills were closing the books, the Pats were just opening them.

The bubbly can wait.

> **"The road to the Super Bowl goes through Foxboro. Everyone knows that."**
>
> —Patriots defensive lineman
> Richard Seymour

Fans taunt ex-Patriots Drew Bledsoe and Lawyer
Milloy during the game against their current team, the
Bills. (Matthew West/Boston Herald)

	1st	2nd	3rd	4th	Final
Buffalo	0	0	0	0	0
New England	14	14	0	3	31

SCORING SUMMARY

Qtr	Team	Play		Time
1	Patriots	TD	Graham 1-yd. pass from Brady (Vinatieri kick)	10:50
1	Patriots	TD	B. Johnson 9-yd. pass from Brady (Vinatieri kick)	5:23
2	Patriots	TD	T. Brown 19-yd. pass from Brady (Vinatieri kick)	14:14
2	Patriots	TD	Givens 10-yd. pass from Brady (Vinatieri kick)	3:55
4	Patriots	FG	Vinatieri 24-yd.	12:50

OFFENSE

BILLS

PASSING	COMP	ATT	YDS	TD	INT
Brown	11	14	119	0	1
Bledsoe	12	29	83	0	1

RECEIVING	REC	YDS	TD
Moulds	7	55	0
Campbell	2	44	0
Reed	5	40	0
Moore	1	28	0
Coleman	3	20	0
Morris	1	8	0
Gash	2	6	0
Henry	2	1	0

RUSHING	ATT	YDS	TD
Henry	15	62	0
Morris	4	17	0
Bledsoe	1	3	0

PATRIOTS

PASSING	COMP	ATT	YDS	TD	INT
Brady	21	32	204	4	0
Huard	0	1	0	0	0

RECEIVING	REC	YDS	TD
Givens	7	80	1
Branch	6	58	0
T. Brown	5	52	1
B. Johnson	1	9	1
Fauria	1	4	0
Graham	1	1	1

RUSHING	ATT	YDS	TD
Smith	15	74	0
Faulk	9	26	0
Brady	5	23	0
Centers	4	9	0
Huard	1	-1	0

Rookie receiver Bethel Johnson dives over the
goal line in the first quarter in spite of defenders Nate Clements and No. 51 Takeo Spikes.
(Kuni Takahashi/Boston Herald)

RICHARD SEYMOUR

93 • DEFENSIVE LINEMAN

PR IS PAYING OFF

BY MICHAEL FELGER, BOSTON HERALD

Richard Seymour is not only the most talented player on the Patriots' roster. With all due respect to Tom Brady and Adam Vinatieri, Seymour is also likely to be the Pats' next superstar.

The recognition for Seymour's abilities is certainly starting to increase. Seymour is ranked first among AFC interior defensive linemen in fan balloting for the Pro Bowl, making him a prohibitive favorite to make his second straight trip to Hawaii.

Beyond that, no one on the Pats' roster works harder at marketing himself, and it's paying off. Seymour has his own web site and his own weekly television segment on Fox Sports Net. He appeared on the ESPN game show *HearSay*. He did a stint on the Jim Rome show last week. He's never met a microphone he didn't like.

But what makes Seymour unique is that through all the self-promotion, he never loses the team concept.

"It's always important to market yourself as a player. But the more you win and the more you do your job and stay humble, then good things are going to come your way," he said. "That's what's been happening to me lately. But on this football team, it really doesn't matter to us. The ultimate goal is to get back to where we once were. And we're not there yet. The better individual effort you can give, the better it's going to make the team without sacrificing some of your own personal stuff. It works both ways."

Seymour will probably never put up huge sack totals because of the system he plays in. Unlike Miami's Jason Taylor, for instance, Seymour doesn't line up on the edge and rush the passer every down. In Bill Belichick's two-gap scheme, Seymour is an interior player whose first responsibility is often holding the line of scrimmage.

"It's frustrating at points," he said. "But you just have to keep pushing on and not allow them to sit back there untested. Even though you don't get sacks as interior linemen, if you can add pressure and force him to get the ball away—you can get paid for that, too."

Richard Seymour backs up his self-promotion with his actions on the field.
(Nancy Lane/Boston Herald)

TENNESSEE 14

AFC EAST CHAMPIONSHIP

NEW ENGLAND 17

VINATIERI, PATS GIVE TENNESSEE THE BOOT
"D" holds up down stretch to stop Titans

BY MICHAEL FELGER, BOSTON HERALD

The coldest game in Patriots history turned out to be another knee-knocker. And it had nothing to do with the weather.

Living up to their cardiac reputation, the Pats got a clutch, wobbly, 46-yard field goal from struggling kicker Adam Vinatieri with 4:06 left in the fourth quarter to post a 17-14 win over Tennessee in the divisional playoffs at Gillette Stadium.

"Two years ago is two years ago," said Vinatieri, trying to downplay the obvious comparisons to the Pats' Cinderella 2001 championship season. "This team steps up when we need to."

The win—which wasn't finalized until Titans receiver Drew Bennett failed to come up with a jump ball from Steve McNair at the Pats' 10-yard line with just 1:45 remaining—sent the Pats to the AFC title game for the second time in three years and fourth time in franchise history.

There were scant no-shows in the announced crowd of 68,436, which braved 4-degree temperatures (minus-10 wind chill) at the opening kickoff.

Just prior to the Titans' last-gasp effort, the players in the huddle got a speech from linebacker Willie McGinest.

"He said, 'This is it. This is the AFC title game. Someone has to step up,'" safety Rodney Harrison said. "And that's what we did."

After McNair heaved the ball, Bennett out-leapt Tyrone Poole and had his hands on the ball but bobbled it. Rookie corner Asante Samuel came in to clean up the play and preserve the win.

"That was a tough way to end it," Bennett said. "I should have made that play, but I didn't. It hit both my hands. I out-jumped the DB and I just didn't make the play."

The Pats are now 4-0 in the postseason under Bill Belichick.

"We expected this to be the toughest game of the year, and it was," Belichick said. "We had a lot of different guys step up in a lot of different areas."

While true, the Pats also gave up more plays than many expected them to. And the result was a victory that didn't come easily. The Titans moved the ball all night, picking primarily on Poole, Samuel and rookie safety Eugene Wilson.

Tennessee continued to gain yards when it counted. After Vinatieri's field goal, McNair drove the Titans into the wind and had them at the verge of field goal range before being driven back. The biggest plays for the Pats during the sequence were referees' decisions. The first was an intentional grounding call on McNair and the second was a holding call on Titans tackle Fred Miller. Both were caused by aggressive blitz calls by defensive coordinator Romeo Crennel, who

Adam Vinatieri scores the game-winning 46-yard
field goal over the outstretched hands of the Titans.
(Kuni Takahashi/Boston Herald)

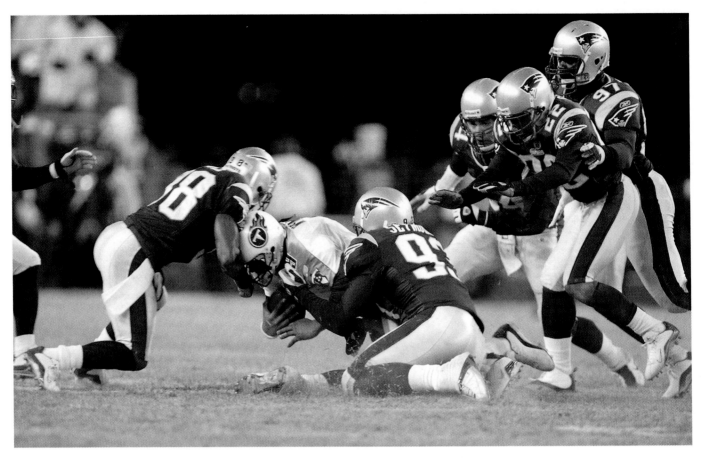

The Patriots' defense pulls down scrambling Titan quarterback Steve McNair in the fourth quarter. (Matthew West/Boston Herald)

determined he couldn't let McNair sit in the pocket and pick his team apart.

Meanwhile, quarterback Tom Brady was masterful in completing 21-of-41 passes for 201 yards and a touchdown (a perfect 41-yard strike to Bethel Johnson on the Pats' opening possession). Had Brady gotten a better game from tight end Daniel Graham, who had a fumble and a huge drop, the Pats' win would have been more comfortable.

"We're not producing as much as I'd like to see, but we're still making the plays at the crucial times," said Brady. "We're still doing a good job making those plays."

The most crucial of those plays came on the game-winning drive. With the Pats facing a fourth-and-3 at the Tennessee 33-yard line with 5:14 on the clock, they went for the first down instead of trying to pooch a punt deep.

The move paid off, as Brady hit Troy Brown with an out pattern just beyond the stakes. A few plays later, Vinatieri hit the game winner.

"Looking back at that kick—those yards came in handy," Brown said.

Indeed, Vinatieri had determined in pregame warmups that his range heading in that direction would be around 48 yards. That looked to be a little shaky in the first quarter, when he hooked a 44-yard attempt wide left.

But in true Patriots fashion, Vinatieri made the kick that counted—even though it was 2 yards longer and in an infinitely tougher situation than the one he missed earlier.

Another day, another dollar for the ultra-clutch Pats.

"Whatever it is we have to do, I feel like we can do it," linebacker Tedy Bruschi said.

Bruschi was asked if there was anything more he could ask for.

"The trophy," he said. "We want to be the last team standing."

"We expected this to be the toughest game of the year, and it was. We had a lot of different guys step up in a lot of different areas."

—Patriots coach Bill Belichick

Bethel Johnson looks the ball into his hands and makes the catch for the first touchdown of the game. (Matthew West/Boston Herald)

	1st	2nd	3rd	4th	Final
Tennessee	7	0	7	0	14
New England	7	7	0	3	17

SCORING SUMMARY

Qtr	Team	Play		Time
1	Patriots	TD	B. Johnson 41-yd. pass from Brady (Vinatieri kick)	10:59
1	Titans	TD	Brown 5-yd. run (Anderson kick)	7:31
2	Patriots	TD	Smith 1-yd. run (Vinatieri kick)	13:46
3	Titans	TD	Mason 11-yd. pass from McNair (Anderson kick)	4:14
4	Patriots	FG	Vinatieri 46-yd.	4:06

OFFENSE

TITANS

PASSING	COMP	ATT	YDS	TD	INT
McNair	18	26	210	1	1

RECEIVING	REC	YDS	TD
Mason	7	90	1
Bennett	3	48	0
Calico	1	30	0
McCareins	2	21	0
Wycheck	2	9	0
George	2	7	0
Kinney	1	5	0

RUSHING	ATT	YDS	TD
George	16	48	0
Brown	7	35	1
McNair	2	11	0
Wycheck	1	-10	0

PATRIOTS

PASSING	COMP	ATT	YDS	TD	INT
Brady	21	41	201	1	0

RECEIVING	REC	YDS	TD
B. Johnson	2	55	1
Fauria	3	42	0
Faulk	3	31	0
Givens	4	26	0
Ward	1	22	0
T. Brown	2	11	0
Branch	3	10	0
Centers	1	4	0
Smith	1	1	0
Graham	1	-1	0

RUSHING	ATT	YDS	TD
Smith	16	69	1
Faulk	5	22	0
Brady	5	5	0
Centers	1	0	0

Antowain Smith breaks free in the third to get the Pats out of a hole deep in their own territory. (Michael Seamans/Boston Herald)

TITANS JUST GOT FREEZER BURNED

True-blue fans cheer for the Patriots during the first-half action against Tennessee. (Kuni Takahashi/Boston Herald)

JANUARY 18, 2004 • GILLETTE STADIUM

INDIANAPOLIS 14
AFC CHAMPIONSHIP
NEW ENGLAND 24

STUFF OF LEGENDS
Homeland Defense secures Super trip

BY MICHAEL FELGER, BOSTON HERALD

Score another one for the legend of the Patriots' Homeland Defense.

The Pats put another high-profile, nationally hyped offense in its place and in so doing earned a trip to the Super Bowl. The final score in the AFC championship game was Patriots 24, Indianapolis 14—but the statement made on the snow-specked field at Gillette Stadium was louder than the numbers.

And we've all heard it before.

Offense wins games. Defense wins championships.

"That was awesome," said coach Bill Belichick, minutes after earning a thunderous ovation from the overflow crowd of 68,436 after being handed the Lamar Hunt Trophy at midfield. "My hat is off to our football players. They played a great game and they played against a great team."

Added special teams captain Larry Izzo: "We're going to H-Town, baby!"

"It's just a great group of young men who work together as a team," said owner Robert Kraft, holding the Lamar Hunt Trophy in the postgame locker room. "I hope we go get the real trophy in two weeks."

The Pats are now 4-0 lifetime in AFC title games. They are also 5-0 in the postseason under Belichick. But as impressive as those numbers are, the talk for the next few days will be centered around how the Pats buried yet another high-scoring attack on football's big stage.

As was the case in their Super Bowl upset of the St. Louis Rams two years ago, the Pats disrupted the timing of the Colts' offense through a defensive scheme that was light on blitzes but big on tight coverage and big hits in the secondary. The Pats sent more than four rushers only twice (when they sent five), but thanks to the coverage, Colts quarterback Peyton Manning was flustered enough to throw four interceptions, take four sacks and go home with a dismal 35.5 quarterback rating.

Cornerback Ty Law was the key player in that drama. He recorded three interceptions while holding all-world receiver Marvin Harrison to three catches (one of which he proceeded to fumble away). The Pats' other defensive stars were safety Rodney Harrison (end zone interception, forced fumble, team-high 10 tackles), and defensive lineman Jarvis Green (three sacks).

Manning came into the game with eight touchdowns, no interceptions and a quarterback rating of 156.9 in this postseason. The publicity he generated off those numbers was a driving motivation for the Pats.

"I'm sick and tired of hearing about Peyton Manning and how many points they put up, three-headed monsters and all that stuff," said receiver Troy Brown.

OPPOSITE: Ty Law picks off Peyton Manning, and No. 88 Marvin Harrison is left with empty hands.
(Matthew West/Boston Herald)

132

Antowain Smith drags the Colts' No. 20, Mike Doss, for extra yards in the first half. Smith rushed for 100 yards on the night. (Kuni Takahashi/Boston Herald)

"I think everybody in this locker room was tired of hearing about the Colts. It was almost sickening."

Did the Patriots feel Manning was flustered?

"You'd have to ask him, but how many interceptions did he throw?" said linebacker Tedy Bruschi. "That's rattled."

Linebacker Willie McGinest added: "The game plan was to bloody their nose a little bit."

The game should have been a blowout, but one of the Pats' big problems during the season, red zone offense, reared its ugly head. They scored only one touchdown on seven trips inside the 20.

Tom Brady (22-of-37 for 237 yards and a touchdown) was splendid, except when the Pats got near the goal line. His fourth-quarter end zone interception was his first home pick of the season, but more importantly it forced everyone to sweat out the fourth quarter.

Manning hit tight end Marcus Pollard for a 7-yard touchdown with 2:27 remaining to cut the Pats' lead to

21-14. After an onside kick was recovered by Pats tight end Christian Fauria, Brady gave the fans another scare when he fumbled at the Indy 16-yard line on a naked bootleg. A video review gave the ball back to the Pats, and Adam Vinatieri nailed his fifth field goal of the day, a 34-yarder, to put the game out of reach.

"We had some opportunities that we just didn't take advantage of," said Brady. "It's kind of scary to keep kicking field goals with how explosive that [Colts] offense is."

But it never came back to haunt the Pats, thanks to their Homeland Defense. The Pats finished the year perfect at home (10-0), but like a lot of other numbers, the players won't be paying too much attention to that the next two weeks.

Law was asked if the win was as good as it gets.

"Not yet," he said. "We have one more game to go. This is not the ultimate goal. It's to go to Houston and win."

"The game plan was to bloody their nose a little bit."

—Patriots linebacker Willie McGinest

No. 97 Jarvis Green takes Peyton Manning down in the backfield. Green finished the game with three sacks. (Matthew West/Boston Herald)

	1st	2nd	3rd	4th	Final
Indianapolis	0	0	7	7	14
New England	7	8	6	3	24

SCORING SUMMARY

Qtr	Team	Play		Time
1	Patriots	TD	Givens 7-yd. pass from Brady (Vinatieri kick)	8:16
2	Patriots	FG	Vinatieri 31-yd.	12:44
2	Patriots	FG	Vinatieri 25-yd.	8:06
2	Patriots		Safety	4:08
3	Colts	TD	James 2-yd. run (Vanderjagt kick)	9:44
3	Patriots	FG	Vinatieri 27-yd.	7:20
3	Patriots	FG	Vinatieri 21-yd.	1:32
4	Colts	TD	Pollard 7-yd. pass from Manning (Vanderjagt kick)	2:27
4	Patriots	FG	Vinatieri 34-yd.	0:50

OFFENSE

COLTS

PASSING	COMP	ATT	YDS	TD	INT
Manning	23	47	237	1	4

RECEIVING	REC	YDS	TD
Pollard	6	90	1
Wayne	4	46	0
Walters	3	30	0
Stokley	3	22	0
Harrison	3	19	0
Rhodes	2	17	0
James	2	13	0

RUSHING	ATT	YDS	TD
James	19	78	1
Rhodes	3	16	0
Manning	2	4	0
Smith	1	0	0

PATRIOTS

PASSING	COMP	ATT	YDS	TD	INT
Brady	22	37	237	1	1

RECEIVING	REC	YDS	TD
T. Brown	7	88	0
Givens	8	68	1
Centers	1	28	0
Branch	2	23	0
Faulk	1	8	0
Fauria	1	8	0
Smith	1	8	0
B. Johnson	1	6	0

RUSHING	ATT	YDS	TD
Smith	22	100	0
Faulk	3	8	0
B. Johnson	1	3	0
Brady	5	1	0
Centers	1	0	0

Troy Brown, in the third quarter, steps in front of
Donald Strickland and pulls in one of his seven catches.
(Matthew West/Boston Herald)

It took a herd of Colts to corral Ty Law
after his third and final interception.
(Matthew West/Boston Herald)

Owner Bob Kraft and quarterback Tom Brady share a warm moment during the AFC championship award ceremony. (Kuni Takahashi/Boston Herald)

A Patriots' fan braves the snow to show her true colors.
(Kuni Takahashi/Boston Herald)

Fans celebrate and fireworks are lit after the Patriots defeated the Colts for the AFC championship. (David Goldman/Boston Herald)

FEBRUARY 1, 2004 • RELIANT STADIUM

NEW ENGLAND 32
SUPER BOWL XXXVIII
CAROLINA 29

BRADY, PATS MAKE IT TWO OUT OF THREE
Vinatieri boots another game winner for second Super Bowl title

BY MICHAEL FELGER, BOSTON HERALD

It just couldn't have happened any other way for Tom Brady, Adam Vinatieri and the New England Patriots.

In yet another clutch, gut-wrenching performance that will only cement the legend of the Pats' quarterback and his historic team, Brady and the Patriots claimed their second NFL championship in three years with a 32-29 victory over the Carolina Panthers in Super Bowl XXXVIII at Houston's Reliant Stadium.

And just like two years ago when the Pats upset St. Louis, it was Brady and Vinatieri who got the job done when it counted, as Brady drove 37 yards in six plays with 1:08 remaining and Vinatieri won it with a 41-yard field goal that split the uprights with four seconds left on the clock.

"It's never easy, is it?" Brady said amid the chaos of the Pats' postgame locker room. While six other quarterbacks are headed to Hawaii to play in the Pro Bowl, Brady, who was voted the game's MVP, is looking ahead to a more legitimate competition. He's not going to Disney World.

"I'm going to Pebble Beach," he said in reference to the Pro-Am golf tournament. "I've got to get ready to win that thing."

Typical. Brady's coolness under pressure and obsession with competition had everyone in the organization shaking their heads in amazement. And it also had owner Robert Kraft making the rounds through the locker room clutching the Vince Lombardi Trophy.

"Is this special or what?" he said. "This is addictive. This is why we bought the team—right here."

The Pats earned a place in the NFL history books with the win, as they became the first team to close out the season with 15 straight victories since the perfect 1972 Dolphins.

But when historians look back at the game, they will focus on Brady and the dramatic final moments of one of the greatest Super Bowls ever played. The Pats led early in the fourth quarter by a 21-10 score when the fireworks started. Carolina running back DeShaun Foster answered with a 33-yard scoring run with 12:39 remaining. Then, with 6:53 left in the game, Carolina's cardiac quarterback, Jake Delhomme, hit Muhsin Muhammad with an 85-yard scoring bomb to put the Panthers in the lead, 22-21.

That marked the first time the Pats had trailed in a game since Nov. 23 (also at Reliant Stadium, against

OPPOSITE: After kicking the game-winning field goal in the final seconds of regulation, Adam Vinatieri is mobbed by holder Ken Walter (No. 13) and Christian Fauri (No. 88). (Kuni Takahashi/Boston Herald)

Quarterback Tom Brady is pumped after gaining a hard-earned first down.
(Matthew West/Boston Herald)

the Texans). But it didn't last long, as Brady engineered an 11-play, 68-yard drive that culminated in a 1-yard touchdown pass to linebacker Mike Vrabel with 2:51 left. A two-point conversion run by Kevin Faulk made it 29-22. But Delhomme had an answer, taking advantage of injuries to starting Pats safeties Rodney Harrison (broken arm) and Eugene Wilson (groin pull) and driving the Panthers to a tying score—a 12-yard pass to Ricky Proehl with 1:08 left.

Carolina kicker John Kasay then committed the cardinal sin, sending the ensuing kickoff out of bounds. Starting at his own 40, Brady drove the Pats down to the Carolina 23-yard line—with the key play being a 17-yard strike to Deion Branch on third-and-3. Vinatieri then drilled home the game winner.

It was vintage Vinatieri, who had an awful game to that point (one missed field goal, one blocked field goal and a muffed squib kick). But once again, he came through when it counted.

"It's a pretty darned good feeling," said Vinatieri. "We deserve it."

It was also vintage Brady, who set a Super Bowl record by completing 32 passes. He finished with 354 yards and three touchdowns (plus one end zone interception), but it was his play in the fourth quarter that once again defined his performance. The 26-year-old

Brady is now the youngest player ever to win multiple Super Bowl MVP awards.

"Here's the quote I want you to print," said team vice chairman Jonathan Kraft. "You beat Peyton Manning twice. You beat Steve McNair twice. You do what he did tonight, and you deserve to be MVP of the league. Period. Tom should have been the MVP. Did you watch how cool he was? He absolutely [sweats] ice cubes."

Added personnel director Scott Pioli: "He knows how to win. He knows how to keep his composure. Stop comparing him to Joe Montana. He's Tom Brady!"

When it was over, Pats players, some of them in tears, poured onto the field as coach Bill Belichick's favorite act, Bon Jovi, poured over the stadium speakers.

"This team met all comers this year," said Belichick. "Fifteen straight. There's been some heart attacks, but they came out on top."

The Pats are now the first team this decade to win multiple championships. The feat will spark legitimate talk all off season about whether the Pats have a dynasty in the making.

"It's just tremendous satisfaction," Pioli said. "As much as anything, it's encouraging for the future. It confirms what we believe in. And we'll just try and do it again."

No. 54 Tedy Bruschi and the Pats' defense stuff Panthers running back Stephen Davis.
(Michael Seamans/Boston Herald)

	1st	2nd	3rd	4th	Final
Carolina	0	10	0	19	29
New England	0	14	0	18	32

SCORING SUMMARY

Qtr	Team	Play	....	Time
2	Patriots	TD	Branch 5-yd. pass from Brady (Vinatieri kick)	3:05
2	Panthers	TD	Smith 39-yd. pass from Delhomme (Kasay kick)	1:07
2	Patriots	TD	Givens 5-yd. pass from Brady (Vinatieri kick)	0:18
2	Panthers	FG	Kasay 50-yd.	0:00
4	Patriots	TD	Smith 2-yd. run (Vinatieri kick)	14:49
4	Panthers	TD	Foster 33-yd. run (Failed 2-pt. conv. attempt)	12:39
4	Panthers	TD	Muhammad 85-yd. pass from Delhomme (Failed 2-pt. conv. attempt)	6:53
4	Patriots	TD	Vrabel 1-yd. pass from Brady (2-pt. conv. succeeds)	2:51
4	Panthers	TD	Proehl 12-yd. pass from Delhomme (Kasay kick)	1:08
4	Patriots	FG	Vinatieri 41-yd.	0:04

OFFENSE

PANTHERS

PASSING	COMP	ATT	YDS	TD	INT
Delhomme	16	33	323	3	0

RECEIVING	REC		YDS		TD
Muhammad	4		140		1
Smith	4		80		1
Proehl	4		71		1
Wiggins	2		21		0
Foster	1		9		0
Mangum	1		2		0

RUSHING	ATT		YDS		TD
Davis	13		49		0
Foster	3		43		1

PATRIOTS

PASSING	COMP	ATT	YDS	TD	INT
Brady	32	48	354	3	1

RECEIVING	REC		YDS		TD
Branch	10		143		1
T. Brown	8		76		0
Givens	5		69		1
Graham	4		46		0
Faulk	4		19		0
Vrabel	1		1		1

RUSHING	ATT		YDS		TD
Smith	26		83		1
Faulk	6		42		0
Brady	2		12		0
T. Brown	1		-10		0

Deion Branch runs away from the defender to score on a 5-yard pass in the second quarter. (Matthew West/Boston Herald)

Tom Brady celebrates the first touchdown of the game, a 5-yard pass to Deion Branch with just over three minutes left in the first half. (Kuni Takahashi/Boston Herald)

"It's a pretty darned good feeling. We deserve it."

—Patriots kicker Adam Vinatieri

Coach Belichick congratulates kicker Adam Vinatieri after his winning field goal as they run off the field. (Nancy Lane/Boston Herald)

Nose tackle Ted Washington howls with joy at the end of regulation. (David Goldman/Boston Herald)

Patriots fans clamor to hold the championship trophy after the game. (Kuni Takahashi/ Boston Herald)

SUPERSTAR BRADY SHINES
Second crown elevates QB to legend status

BY KAREN GUREGIAN, BOSTON HERALD

If someone were to sculpt a Mount Rushmore of Boston sports legends, the faces of Ted Williams, Bill Russell, Bobby Orr and Larry Bird would hold some serious rock space.

Prior to last night, there would be no Patriot players etched in stone. There would be no football representatives getting face time on our pretend mountain.

After the Patriots' 32-29 win over the Carolina Panthers, however, a case can be made for a new entry in that special pantheon—a Patriots entry.

Tom Brady has now captured two Super Bowl MVPs and has engineered two clutch and heroic last-minute drives to set up Adam Vinatieri for a pair of championship-winning field goals. Twice now in three seasons, he has delivered the goods on the largest stage.

Brady may not be in that rare stratosphere with Williams, Russell, Orr and Bird in terms of pure talent and ability. It can certainly be argued that he doesn't single-handedly dominate games like the above collection of greats did in their respective sports for so many years, and he is not yet considered the best at his position.

But Brady owns two very important qualities possessed by our sacred stars. He wins. He is now 6-0 in the playoffs with a pair of rings. And in terms of sheer star power and popularity in New England and beyond, he's godlike, just like those giants of the past.

Brady's performance last night merely solidified his celebrity and probably multiplied it by the number on his jersey.

He had played a near perfect game before throwing a fourth-quarter interception that gave the Panthers life and put them back in the game. Up by five, Brady had a third-and-9 from the Panther 9, and found Reggie Howard—not Christian Fauria—in the end zone.

But like a true superstar, the Super Bowl at stake with the final ticks of the clock, Brady calmly led the team into field goal range after taking over from the Pats' 40. Against the St. Louis Rams two years ago, he worked his magic with 1:21 on the clock. This time, he had 68 seconds to move Vinatieri into range and break the deadlock to win the game before overtime.

After an incomplete pass to Deion Branch, he hit Troy Brown for 13 yards. A pass interference call negated a 20-yard completion to Brown and pushed the Pats back. Undaunted, Brady hit Brown for 13, Daniel Graham for 4, and then Branch for 17 yards on a third-and-3 from the Carolina 40 to set up Vinatieri for his game-winning 41-yarder with four seconds left.

"I think we realized we had done it sometimes this year, to make plays like that [during crunch time]," Brady said. "It's something we work on all the time in practice, something that we're trying to execute as well as we can. We just made enough plays."

In all, Brady was masterful, completing 32-of-48 passes for 354 yards with three touchdown passes and the one pick.

Brady may feel uncomfortable with all the comparisons to Hall of Famer Joe Montana; he may even feel completely unworthy, but if he continues to rack up Super Bowl wins and Super Bowl MVPs, it'll be hard not to justify them.

"He threw a touchdown to win [a Super Bowl]. I haven't thrown a touchdown to win it," Brady said, once again downplaying the comparisons to the 49er great. "He's the benchmark for quarterbacks in this league. The way he played under pressure, and the way he succeeded and thrived in tight situations, he was an incredible player. There's no way I'm even close to that. It's my fourth year. And I think we're still trying to make better plays and better reads. Hopefully, one day I'm on that level, but no way now."

At the very least, he's a budding Montana and a budding superstar who may leave us no choice but to get the chisel out and put him alongside Boston's other legends. Mount Rushmore awaits.

OPPOSITE: Two-time MVP Tom Brady holds the Lombardi trophy during the awards ceremony. (Matthew West/Boston Herald)

PATRIOTS REGULAR SEASON STATISTICS

OFFENSE

Passing

PLAYER	COMP	ATT	YDS	PCT	TD	INT
Brady	317	527	3620	60.2	23	12
Davey	3	7	31	42.9	0	0
Givens	0	1	0	0.0	0	1
Faulk	0	1	0	0.0	0	0
Huard	0	1	0	0.0	0	0

Receiving

PLAYER	REC	YDS	AVG	TD
Branch	57	803	14.1	3
Givens	34	510	15.0	6
T. Brown	40	472	11.8	4
Faulk	48	440	9.2	0
Graham	38	409	10.8	4
Fauria	28	285	10.2	2
B. Johnson	16	209	13.1	2
Patten	9	140	15.6	0
Centers	19	106	5.6	1
Ward	7	106	15.1	1
Smith	14	92	6.6	0
Stokes	2	38	19.0	0
Pass	4	21	5.3	0
McCrary	2	12	6.0	0
Cloud	1	8	8.0	0
Andruzzi	1	0	0.0	0

Rushing

PLAYER	ATT	YDS	AVG	TD
Smith	182	642	3.5	3
Faulk	178	638	3.6	0
Cloud	27	118	4.4	5
Centers	21	82	3.9	0
Brady	42	63	1.5	1
T. Brown	6	27	4.5	0
Pass	6	27	4.5	0
Branch	1	11	11.0	0
Klecko	2	5	2.5	0
Patten	1	4	4.0	0
McCrary	3	3	1.0	0
Walter	2	0	0.0	0
Huard	1	-1	-1.0	0
B. Johnson	1	-12	-12.0	0

SPECIAL TEAMS

Field Goals

PLAYER	1-20	20-29	30-39	40-49	50+
Vinatieri	0/0	16/17	4/8	5/8	0/1

Punting

PLAYER	NO	AVG	INSIDE 20
Walter	76	37.7	25
Barnard	10	36.5	4
Brady	1	36	1

Punt Returns

PLAYER	ATT	YDS	FC	AVG	TD
T. Brown	29	293	13	10.1	0
Poole	11	75	3	6.8	0
Faulk	5	66	6	13.2	0
Branch	4	26	1	6.5	0
B. Johnson	1	2	0	2.0	0

Kickoff Returns

PLAYER	ATT	YDS	AVG	TD
B. Johnson	30	847	28.2	1
Pass	11	254	23.1	0
Faulk	10	207	20.7	0
Cloud	2	38	19.0	0
Givens	2	31	15.5	0
Klecko	2	20	10.0	0
Vrabel	2	22	11.0	0
Bruschi	1	9	9.0	0

DEFENSE

Tackles

PLAYER	NO	SOLO	AST
Bruschi	128	81	47
Harrison	125	94	31
Phifer	100	68	32
Law	74	62	12
McGinest	67	48	19
Wilson	61	48	13
Poole	59	48	11
Seymour	56	37	19
Vrabel	52	37	15
Hamilton	46	32	14

PLAYER	NO	SOLO	AST		PLAYER	NO
Washington	40	33	7		Harrison	3
Warren	33	20	13		Bruschi	2
Samuel	32	29	3		Colvin	2
Chatham	21	15	6		Green	2
T. Johnson	21	15	6		Washington	2
Green	17	9	8		Chatham	1.5
Klecko	17	12	5		Klecko	1.5
Harris	10	6	4		Banta-Cain	1
Lyle	9	7	2		Cherry	1
Akins	8	4	4		Pleasant	1
Colvin	5	3	2		Warren	1
Izzo	5	5	0			
Cherry	4	4	0			
Mayer	3	3	0			
Banta-Cain	2	1	1			
Davis	1	1	0			
Pleasant	1	1	0			

Sacks

PLAYER	NO
Vrabel	9.5
Seymour	8
McGinest	5.5

Interceptions

PLAYER	INT	YDS	AVG	TD
Law	6	112	18.0	1
Poole	6	81	13.0	0
Wilson	4	18	4.0	0
Bruschi	3	26	8.0	2
Harrison	3	0	0.0	0
Samuel	2	55	27.0	1
Vrabel	2	18	9.0	0
Izzo	1	0	0.0	0
McGinest	1	15	15.0	1
Morris	1	33	33.0	0

TEAM

	PATRIOTS	OPP
Touchdowns	38	23
Passing	23	11
Rushing	9	10
Defensive	6	2
First downs	281	286
Passing	170	172
Rushing	86	89
Penalty	25	25
3rd down: made/att	79/209	77/217
Net yards passing	3282	3198
Net yards rushing	1529	1358

The entire staff of the *Boston Herald* photography department contributed to the coverage of the New England Patriots' 2003-04 season, which culminated in a Super Bowl victory. We gratefully acknowledge the efforts of staff photographers:

Michael Adaskaveg
Tara Bricking
Stuart Cahill
Renee DeKona
Robert Eng
Michael Fein
Ted Fitzgerald
Mark Garfinkel
David Goldman
Jonathon Hill
Nancy Lane
George Martell
Faith Ninivaggi
Michael Seamans
Matt Stone
Kuni Takahashi
Matthew West
Patrick Whittemore
John Wilcox
Kevin Wisniewski

and

Jim Mahoney, Director of Photography
Ted Ancher, Assistant Director
Arthur Pollock, Assistant Director
John Cummings, Assignment Editor
John Landers, Assignment Editor